MARION DEWAR

A FEMINIST HISTORY SOCIETY BOOK

MARION DEWAR
A LIFE of ACTION

by
DEBORAH GORHAM

Second Story Press

Library and Archives Canada Cataloguing in Publication

Gorham, Deborah, author
Marion Dewar : a life of action / by Deborah Gorham.

(A Feminist History Society book)
Issued in print and electronic formats.
ISBN 978-1-77260-009-4 (paperback).–ISBN 978-1-77260-033-9 (hardback)
ISBN 978-1-77260-010-0 (epub)

1. Dewar, Marion, 1928-2008. 2. Mayors–Ontario–Ottawa–Biography.
3. New Democratic Party–Biography. 4. Women politicians–Canada–Biography.
5. Social reformers–Canada–Biography. 6. Ottawa (Ont.)–Biography. I. Title.
II. Series: Feminist History Society book

FC3096.26.D48G67 2016   971.3'8404092   C2016-903539-5

C2016-903540-9

Editors: Kathryn White and Kathryn Cole
Book design by Melissa Kaita
Original series design by Zab Design & Typography

The poem "The Place Where We Are Right" by Yehuda Amichai
is used with kind permission of University of California Press.

All royalties earned by this book will be divided between the Marion Dewar
Scholarship Fund of the Ottawa Community Immigrant Services Organization
and Oxfam Canada's Marion Dewar Fund for Women's Leadership.

Every effort has been made to secure permission and provide appropriate
credit for photographic material. The publisher deeply regrets any omission
and pledges to correct errors called to its attention in subsequent editions.

Printed and bound in Canada

*Second Story Press gratefully acknowledges the support of the
Ontario Arts Council and the Canada Council for the Arts for our
publishing program. We acknowledge the financial support of the
Government of Canada through the Canada Book Fund.*

ONTARIO ARTS COUNCIL
CONSEIL DES ARTS DE L'ONTARIO
an Ontario government agency
un organisme du gouvernement de l'Ontario

Canada Council   Conseil des Arts
for the Arts   du Canada

Funded by the Government of Canada
Financé par le gouvernement du Canada

Canadä

Published by
Second Story Press
20 Maud Street, Suite 401
Toronto, ON M5V 2M5
www.secondstorypress.ca

To Toby Gelfand, with love and thanks

CONTENTS

I   INTRODUCTION

11   CHAPTER 1
Beginnings

37   CHAPTER 2
A Suburban Housewife?

63   CHAPTER 3
Entering Public Life

79   CHAPTER 4
Her Worship

115   CHAPTER 5
Federal Politics

135 CONCLUSION

141 *Appendix*

143 *References*

153 *Index*

163 *Acknowledgements*

167 *Photo Credits*

169 *About the Author*

INTRODUCTION

Marion Dewar is best remembered as mayor of Ottawa. Many people (myself included) believe she was the best mayor Ottawa has ever had. From 1978 to 1985, Mayor Dewar worked for non-profit housing, better public transportation, and support for the arts, peace, and women's rights. She advocated for First Nations people, and she supported the revitalization of Ottawa's downtown core. Dewar's advocacy for all these causes, but most especially for peace and women's rights, drew me to her as a subject for a biography.

Dewar's success as mayor, important as it was, is only part of her legacy. Marion Dewar cared deeply about social issues, the poor, and the disadvantaged. She would never ignore a man or woman who was begging in the street, and she not only gave money but also words of encouragement and friendship. When she encountered those in need, she would reach out to help them – other more "important" people could wait. She was a genuinely compassionate woman.

Moreover, Dewar truly did think globally and act locally. While she was mayor, Ottawa became the first municipality in Canada to pass a referendum on global disarmament. She advocated for mothers who lived in public housing, for visible minorities, and for gays and lesbians. And she was the driving force behind Project 4000, an initiative that aimed to bring 4,000 boat people to Ottawa from Vietnam and elsewhere in Southeast Asia.

Dewar was a prominent member of the New Democratic Party (NDP), serving as president of the federal party from 1985 to 1987 and then sitting as a Member of Parliament (MP) for the federal riding of Hamilton-Mountain in 1987–1988. She worked to raise the consciousness of party members about women's political rights and was one of the most important backers of MP Audrey McLaughlin's successful bid for the party leadership.

Describing how Marion Dewar achieved these goals is a major purpose of this book. But how did she come to believe in these issues? What intellectual paths and personal experiences led to her belief in inclusiveness, in the rights of women, in social welfare, in peace?

Passion, pragmatism, and hard work fuelled Dewar's success. Her public actions speak for themselves. Unfortunately for the historian, however, she did not record her personal beliefs. Unlike Audrey McLaughlin, for example, she left behind no memoir. Nor are there diaries or collections of intellectually revealing letters, and while she gave some powerful speeches as mayor, they represent collaboration between her and her staff. The most personally revealing document I encountered in the course of my research is the extraordinary interview conducted by researcher Greta Hofmann Nemiroff in the mid-1990s.[1]

Marion Dewar had strong beliefs on which she had the courage to act, but she was never much interested in abstract, theoretical approaches to ideas. Did her belief in social justice rest upon her Catholic faith? On women and peace, did she believe that women have a gift for consensus and a special responsibility to oppose war and violence? In what follows, I speculate about these questions, but I cannot provide definitive answers. What is clear is that Dewar gave considerable thought to her actions, but for her it was the actions that counted.

By the early 1970s, when her public life began, Marion Dewar identified herself as a supporter of women's rights. Later she would call herself a feminist, and she was identified as such by others. But what kind of feminist was she? What circumstances led her to advocate for an end to discrimination against women in public life and to fight the oppression that women all too often experienced within the family, as mothers and wives?

The 1960s and 1970s saw a revival of feminism. Many women "discovered" feminism for the first time. I was a feminist before the revival of the 1960s and 1970s because I was raised in a mid-twentieth-century feminist family with a working mother who had a satisfying, well-paying job. My mother was forthright about her feminism, and she made it clear to my sister and me that we needed to rely on ourselves and prepare ourselves to earn a living and that we must never think we should be dependent on a man.

But I was profoundly affected by the feminism of the 1960s and 1970s. I read groundbreaking books like Kate Millett's *Sexual Politics*. I began to teach women's history and women's studies and to write about women in history. I was fortunate: As a professor at Carleton University, I earned a living doing work to which I was deeply committed.

Before I began this project, I assumed – wrongly – that Dewar became a feminist during the revival of feminism, as so many other women did. In fact, her transformation from a girl who accepted patriarchal gender divisions to a woman who advocated for women's rights came about in surprising ways. She does not fit the "standard framework." She was not reading *Sexual Politics* in the 1970s.

The standard framework was developed by thinkers confronted with the challenge of providing a narrative through which nineteenth- and early twentieth-century feminism, as well the revival of feminism in the 1960s to 1980s, could be understood. The framework is both useful and generally accepted. The flowering of the 1960s and 1970s has become known as "second wave" feminism. Writers on Canadian second wave feminism acknowledge international influences, especially those coming from the United States. But most also discuss the fragmentation of the movement in Canada, which, as Roberta Hamilton puts it, "was never a single organization, and much of it was never organized in the more traditional sense."[2] Hamilton (like most other writers on this subject) does distinguish between two paths to feminism in Canada: liberal feminism on the one hand, and radical feminism on the other. Liberal feminism is the formal, organized movement to secure legal, social, cultural, and economic justice for women from the Canadian state. Hamilton, an insightful and nuanced thinker, emphasizes the radicalism imbedded in liberal feminism. A key document for Canada's liberal feminists was the report of the Royal Commission on the Status of Women (1972). The Commission recommended ending women's poverty,

A gift to Mayor Dewar when she was about to leave office, in 1985.

developing a national plan for daycare, and modifying the laws prohibiting abortion. Almost half a century later, we still have not achieved these goals. As Hamilton points out, without radical changes to politics and to the structure of the workplace and the family, they never will be achieved. For Hamilton, in consequence, radicalism is inevitably imbedded in liberal feminism.

In 1971, the National Action Committee on the Status of Women (NAC) was formed. In their history of NAC, Jill Vickers, Pauline Rankin, and Christine Appelle emphasize that in its early years NAC represented "radical liberalism" and was an "umbrella group" that was also able to include socialist feminists and the "new feminism."[3]

In contrast to Hamilton and to Vickers et al, other Canadian feminists, most notably Nancy Adamson, Linda Briskin, and Margaret McPhail, emphasize the limitations as opposed to the radicalism of liberal feminism.[4] In *Feminist Organizing for Change*, the authors divide Canadian feminism into liberal, grassroots, and socialist branches. The divisions are clear and easy to understand, but they are too tidy. There was more of an overlap between variet-ies of feminism in the 1960s to 1980s than these categories suggest.

What, then, was women's liberation or grassroots feminism or "new" feminism? What did it mean in Canada? The late Robin Williams once said, "If you remember the 60s you weren't there."[5] Williams was referring to the "sex, drugs, and rock and roll" side of the 1960s youth revolt. But the revolt also had powerful political sides, and they included women's liberation, which manifested itself through the emergence of consciousness-raising groups, study groups, and women's centres in Canada as well as the United States. Most of the women involved in women's liberation in North America were young – in their late teens or twenties – and politically on the left, and their goal was to transform all aspects of society. They especially wanted to challenge the norms of the post-war traditional family. They wanted women to have full reproductive rights, and they demonstrated for abortion on demand. Their most visible action

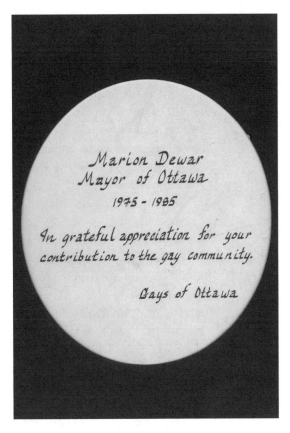

Another tribute for Mayor Dewar, upon leaving office in 1985.

was the Abortion Caravan, which travelled from Vancouver to Ottawa in the spring of 1970. As the Vancouver Women's Caucus stated, "We consider the government of Canada is in a state of war with the women of Canada. If steps are not taken to implement our demands by Monday, May 11, 1970…we will be forced to respond by declaring war on the Canadian government."[6]

In 1970, Marion Dewar was not "declaring war on the Canadian government," nor is there any evidence that in 1972 she was reading the report of the Royal Commission on the Status of Women. Nonetheless, second wave feminism was very much part of the milieu in which Dewar's political career played out, and we can surmise that it had an influence on her, even if that influence was not direct.

Dewar's primary attachments in 1970 were to the Catholic Church, to her profession of nursing, to her family, and to those around her who were in need – both neighbours and members of the wider community.

Born in 1928, and having had a traditional marriage in the 1960s, Dewar was in fact too old for women's liberation, and the circumstances of her life were too traditional. (On the other hand, she certainly was young enough to be a Canadian liberal feminist. Florence Bird, Chair of the Royal Commission on the Status of Women, was born in 1908.) It was her son Bob who was involved in rebellion in the 1960s. She was involved not as a participant but as a parent.

We certainly know something about Dewar's early life and her married life in the 1950s and 1960s, subjects I take up in chapters 1 and 2. Born Marion Bell, she grew up in Buckingham, Quebec, where she was educated at a Catholic primary school and a Protestant high school. She completed grade 13 at Glebe Collegiate Institute in Ottawa. After grade 13, she trained as a nurse, graduating in 1949 from St. Joseph's School of Nursing at the Hotel Dieu Hospital in Kingston. She then nursed at the Ottawa Civic Hospital, and it was there that she met Ken Dewar, a public servant, who was a patient at the Civic. They fell in love and were married in 1951.

The Dewars, like the Bells, were Roman Catholic. After a brief period in which she worked full-time with the Victorian Order of Nurses, Marion and Ken began their family. They had four children, and until the youngest was ready for school, Marion reduced the hours she worked as a nurse. She did volunteer work and in the late 1960s she went back to school, earning a certificate and a degree in public health from the University of Ottawa.

During these years, significant changes were taking place in the Roman Catholic Church. When Pope John XXIII was elected in 1958, he was expected to be a caretaker. Instead, in 1962, he called the reformist Second Vatican Council (which would complete its work in 1965). As far as women's rights within the church were concerned, the Second Vatican Council changed little: Priests still had to be men, birth control was still prohibited, abortion was anathema, and God was still God the Father. But the council did agree that the church should become more accessible. Mass was to be said in the vernacular, rather than in Latin. When saying Mass, the priest was to face the congregation rather than the altar, and there was to be more participation of the laity including women.

Throughout her life Marion Dewar was a devout Roman Catholic, and in her early years she was a Catholic who did not question the authority of the Church hierarchy. However, over the years her faith evolved and she became an outspoken and critical member of the church, supporting contraception, a woman's right to choose abortion, and the ordination of women (the "litmus test," according to radical feminist theologian Mary Daly, for radical change concerning women within the church).[7] While Marion Dewar insisted that the Catholic Church was her church, and she would remain faithful to it, some Catholics were scandalized by her radicalism. Others, like the extraordinary priests at St. Basil's Church, her parish in Ottawa, protected her from censure.

Dewar was also influenced by changes within the nursing profession. Nursing historian Susan Gelfand Malka has documented these changes in the context of the United States.[8] Nurses, Malka writes, became more assertive, more convinced that their profession was distinct from that of physicians, and that its autonomy should be recognized. Malka argues that while some nurses embraced feminism before the 1980s, it was Carol Gilligan's *In a Different Voice* (1982) – which first advocated a uniquely feminine ethic of care – that made feminism acceptable to large numbers of nurses. Dewar was an advocate for women by the 1970s, but this advocacy sprang primarily from her commitment to "an ethic of care."

Marion Dewar's career in city government began in 1972 when she was elected alderman for Britannia Ward. In chapters 3, 4, and 5, I focus on her public achievements. Like many feminist scholars, however, I believe that the "personal is political," and so I explore those facets of her beliefs and private experiences that contributed to shaping her public life. How did Dewar define herself as a woman? She combined wifehood and motherhood with a public career. How did she negotiate the complex problems these multiple roles presented?

Dewar succeeded in public life in Canada during a period when such an achievement was still rare for a woman. When she became Britannia Ward's alderman in 1972, she was the only woman among the sixteen elected officials. She then became Ottawa's second woman mayor. The first was Charlotte Whitton, a very different sort of woman: conservative in contrast to the left-leaning Dewar, and confrontational, in contrast to Dewar, who always strived for co-operation.

In 2002, Marion Dewar was appointed a Member of the Order of Canada. She received this honour because of her achievements as mayor of Ottawa, her work for social justice, and her ability to "transcend partisanship."[9] When she died in 2008, New Democrat Ed Broadbent said, "Today we have lost one of our heroes. Marion Dewar was a champion of what was just and right."

*Author's note: In places where I do not provide direct citations for information, the reader may assume that the information came from interviews and email correspondence I had with Marion Dewar's family, friends, and colleagues. See the Appendix for details.

ENDNOTES:

[1] Marion Dewar interview conducted by Greta Hofmann Nemiroff, c. 1995: City of Ottawa Archives, Marion Dewar Fonds, A2010-0767, "Transcripts." Interview conducted as part of a project overseen by Janice Leroux, of the University of Ottawa. Feminist scholar and activist Hofmann Nemiroff, who worked for this project, remembers that she was the interviewer. At that time, she was Joint Chair in Women's Studies at Carleton University – University of Ottawa. Cited as "Hofmann Nemiroff interview."

[2] Roberta Hamilton, *Gendering the Vertical Mosaic: Feminist Perspectives on Canadian Society* (Toronto: Copp Clark, Ltd., 1996), 52–53.

[3] Jill Vickers, Pauline Rankin, and Christine Appelle, *Politics as if Women Mattered: A Political Analysis of the National Action Committee on the Status of Women* (Toronto: University of Toronto Press, 1993), 71 and ff.

[4] Nancy Adamson, Linda Briskin, and Margaret McPhail, *Feminist Organizing for Change: The Contemporary Women's Movement in Canada* (Toronto: Oxford University Press, 1988).

[5] http://nytimes.com/1988/02/07/books/young-werther-in-the-60-s. html Review of Lawrence Wright's *Growing Up With America: 1960-1984* (2/7/1988), accessed June 4, 2016.

[6] Adamson et al., 46.

[7] Mary Daly, *The Church and the Second Sex* (New York: Harper and Row, 1968). This book was the first major religious liberationist feminist text. Daly's remark about the "litmus test" is cited in an article by Edward Maron, *U.S. Catholic*, vol. 34, no. 5 (1968): 21–24.

[8] Susan Gelfand Malka, *Daring to Care: American Nursing and Second-Wave Feminism* (Urbana, IL: University of Illinois Press, 2007).

[9] Marion Dewar, Order of Canada, http://www.gg.ca/honour. aspx?id=8319&t=12&ln=Dewar, accessed June 4, 2016.

Chapter 1
BEGINNINGS

Marion Hilda Bell was born in Montreal on February 17, 1928, and baptized at Montreal's Holy Family Church.[10] She was the third and last child born to Agnes (Cunningham) and Wilson Edward Bell. The Bells' first child, Olive, was born in 1921. She was followed by Wilson Edward III (Ted) in 1924. Both Agnes and Wilson were British immigrants. Each had been poor in childhood, and both were intelligent and resourceful. As a couple they succeeded in shaping a new destiny, rising out of the working class and refashioning themselves as members of the professional middle class.

DEWAR'S PARENTS' EARLY YEARS

Wilson Bell was extraordinarily talented with his hands and with his brain. Although he had little formal education, by 1928 Bell was making his way as an electrician and engineer and garnering sizeable contracts. Bell's work took him all over Canada, and in the summer months his family accompanied him. His biggest opportunity came in the summer of 1929 when he was hired as an electrical installer through the General Electric Company at the mammoth Seven Sisters Dam project north of Winnipeg. His professional success was a remarkable feat. Early twentieth-century Canada did offer opportunities for one to become a self-made man, but Bell's childhood had been heartbreakingly harsh. Born in the North of England in 1899, little Wilson left for Canada with his mother in 1904. At five, he was the youngest of the four children his mother brought with her. When they sailed from Liverpool to Montreal, arriving on October 22, Wilson's sister Hilda was just a year older than he was. Not long after his mother's arrival, she met a new man. The two youngest children were a burden for their mother, given her new circumstances, and she put them in an orphanage. Ted Bell told me that they remained there until their father's sister Ada learned of the situation and travelled from England to rescue them and bring them up. The orphanage they had been taken to was Catholic, because the mother was Catholic, and the language used there was French. By the time Aunt Ada removed the children from the orphanage, little Wilson had forgotten most of his English. Wilson did learn English again quickly – he was an intelligent boy – but he also never forgot his French.[11]

Wilson had to go out to work at fifteen. He got a job at a Montreal hotel as an electrician, though he did not have formal qualifications.[12] It was there that he met his future wife, Agnes Cunningham, who was working at the hotel as a maid. (Ted Bell said she also worked in a munitions factory for some months during the First World War.) In 1914, when she was eighteen, Agnes had emigrated from Scotland to Canada with her sister Ellen. Her sister Bridget had arrived in 1913. Ellen and Bridget, known to family members as Nellie and Cissie, were twins, eight years older than Agnes. The Cunninghams were from Coatbridge, a grim little coal mining community outside Glasgow, and most of them were very poor. In terms of religion, they were, like the Bells, Catholic.[13]

Wilson and Agnes were still teenagers when they had their first date, and soon they were sweethearts. According to an amusing family story, Agnes, who knew no French and would never learn any, worked with French-speaking young women. They mischievously taught her to say this phrase: *Voulez-vous coucher avec moi?* She had no idea that it meant, "Would you like to go to bed with me?" Liz Dewar explained that when she used it on that first date, Wilson, of course, knew what it meant, but he also knew that Agnes did not.

Their romance was interrupted when Wilson joined the Canadian military and went overseas. In 1919 Agnes and her sisters returned to Coatbridge for a visit, and Wilson, still in Britain, travelled to Scotland to meet Agnes's family.[14] Wilson and Agnes were married the following year. The marriage was solemnized in Montreal on September 15, 1920, at St. Dominic's, Wilson Bell's parish church.[15] They settled down in Montreal, where Bell worked at a variety of jobs. When he could he worked as an electrician, although sometimes he did bricklaying, and he was also a chauffeur.

The height of Bell's career came in 1929, when he was hired as an electrical installer for the Seven Sisters Hydro-Electric Dam project. The Seven Sisters were a set of rapids on the Winnipeg River. In the summer of 1929, when Wilson Bell first came out to the Seven Sisters site, his earnings were sufficient to pay for Agnes and the children and her two older sisters to travel back to Scotland for a visit. The seven of them left in June and returned to Montreal in early August. Ted Bell, five years old in 1929, remembers that the family stayed with their father at the Seven Sisters site. Perhaps they all went out there in August of 1929, after their return to Montreal. The Seven Sisters construction camp was situated some ninety miles north of Winnipeg. Ted remembers that there was no hotel "and just a few houses." The Bell family had one of the houses, which set them apart. The ordinary workers lived in tents. But then came the stock market crash in October 1929, which ushered in the Great Depression. The Seven Sisters operation did not escape its effects. The plant was shut down in a hurry and Bell was laid off.

Bell tried to make a living by starting a taxi service, which was not a success. But then he met with great good fortune when a friend recommended him for a job with the MacLaren lumber enterprises in Masson, Quebec. He accepted the offer gratefully and in the early 1930s the family moved from Montreal to the beautiful Lièvre Valley, living for a time in Masson and then moving to Buckingham, the town where Marion Bell grew up.

GROWING UP IN BUCKINGHAM

The Lièvre River rises north of the town of Mont Laurier and flows south for some 250 miles before emptying into the Ottawa River at Masson. The river valley encompasses some 4,800 square miles. Before Europeans settled there, the Algonquin people used the enormous river basin for hunting and fishing but they did not farm.[16] They used the forests, too, but they did not devastate or exploit them. European entrepreneurs and small farmers changed all

Marion Bell as a toddler. C. 1930.

that, although much of the river to the north of Buckingham remains wild and beautiful to this day. The southern reaches, however, were tamed with dams. Extensive lumbering of the massive white and red pine began. By the 1830s there was a lumbering settlement at the present day location of Buckingham. The community was incorporated as a village in 1855.

In the 1930s and 1940s, during Marion's childhood, Buckingham was surrounded by farmland and functioned as the hub for the farmers round about. However it was more than that. Buckingham was in fact a modern town, a product of industrialization. It was a centre for lumber, for the mining of minerals, and for pulp making. It had a complex social structure involving an intricate pattern of economic, social, ethnic, religious, and linguistic divisions. In 1896, there were some 4,000 inhabitants and two major companies, the MacLaren Company and the Electric Reduction Corporation (ERCO), the latter a mining and mineral operation that, at the peak of its success, produced much of the phosphorus used in matches manufactured for the United Kingdom.

Although the Electric Reduction Corporation was an important employer, there is no question that the MacLarens and their enterprises dominated the town during the late nineteenth century and into the early twentieth century. The firm's founder, James MacLaren (1818–1892) settled in Buckingham in 1864. The MacLarens were Scottish Presbyterians. James established a sawmill and later a pulp mill, and the family owned much of the surrounding land, employing most of the male population of the town and adjacent countryside. Unlike the MacLarens, most of the townspeople were French-speaking and Catholic. Historian Jean Louis Lapointe has thoroughly documented the bitter divide between these Scottish lumber barons and the elites, both anglophone and francophone, who depended on them, and the workers who laboured in the winter felling trees in the bush and in the summer at the sawmill. By the early twentieth century, the MacLarens believed, correctly, that they could control the town. They did so by manipulating its governance and its police force. They dammed the Lièvre, wreaking havoc on the environment, and they exploited their workers as well as the forests and the river.

But there were tensions, and they erupted with violence in 1906 when a group of workers tried to organize a union. The MacLarens, with the connivance of the police, broke the union and staged a successful lockout. In a confrontation that took place on October 8, 1906, their agents murdered two of the leading union organizers: "My God, they're shooting to kill," cried Thomas Belanger as he fell to the ground, mortally wounded.[17]

By the early 1930s, when Wilson and Agnes moved first from Montreal to Masson and then to Buckingham with their three children, Buckingham and the Lièvre area had indeed changed; but much had remained the same. The MacLarens never forgot nor forgave the events of 1906. After the defeat of the unionists, the company established a blacklist of men involved in the organization attempt. There were some three hundred names on this list.[18] As a consequence, many families simply had to leave the area because the men could not get work in the bush or at the mill. This blacklist remained a factor until the 1940s. It probably lessened the hostility to the MacLarens in the town, because so many dissidents were forced to leave. But like the MacLarens, many townspeople did not forget.

Meanwhile, the Electric Reduction Corporation grew in the period after the First World War. MacLarens fought and lost a legal battle with ERCO in 1923. The case concerned the damming of the Lièvre River. The MacLarens never expected to lose, and in retaliation against ERCO, the MacLarens forced their management employees to accept a "social boycott," instructing them to shun ERCO executives. This social deep-freeze, which lasted more than a decade, ended when MacLaren's president married the only daughter of ERCO's president. On the day of the wedding, Allan

Todd told me "all the Buckingham bells rang out." As these tensions indicate, in the 1920s and the years that followed, ERCO became a countervailing force in the community.[19]

Wilson Bell was initially hired to work on the hydro-electric plant the MacLarens constructed at Masson. He spent the rest of his working life with the firm, retiring when he was seventy. By the early 1930s he had become an executive at MacLarens, and for much of his career he was the company's chief engineer. As Ted Bell said, "There were…the manufacturers, the priests, and the doctors. And just below them were people like my father."

UPWARD MOBILITY:
BECOMING PILLARS OF THE COMMUNITY
The Bells lived in several houses in Buckingham, the most attractive being the one that would dominate Marion's childhood. It was a spacious house on Main Street, with a curved front staircase. The Bells were also able to employ a maid. In short, they had become pillars of the community. A fine house did add to a family's status during this period, and so did hiring domestic help, but a house and a maid do not in themselves produce a successful social transformation. That requires changes to an individual's and a family's style of life. Wilson Bell's talents and drive were fundamental to the family's rise in status but, not surprisingly, it was Agnes who created the family's new style.

As historical sociologist Leonore Davidoff has pointed out in her analysis of Victorian England's social structure, changing a family's style of life was, for the most part, the work of women. It remained so in the twentieth century.[20] Ted, who loved his mother dearly, remarked to me, "She'd been just a maid, remember, very poor." But when Wilson Bell began to do well, she was determined to raise her own social status and that of the family. "I don't know how she did it…but she took on the language and the manners of a cultivated woman. She was always a lady." Agnes learned to play golf and to curl. She volunteered for the Red Cross and was active on its Buckingham board.

In 1995, commenting late in life about the social status of her family of origin, Dewar told interviewer Greta Hofmann Nemiroff that she was, in retrospect, fully aware of the fact that her parents were committed to raising the family's status. "My parents were… very upwardly mobile. They were ambitious. It would be naïve to think they weren't…. And they wanted us to be of a different social class than they saw themselves as children." Still, according to Marion, they were never entirely secure: "My mother worked in the Red Cross…but she used to give me the reports and ask me to read them to see if there were any mistakes in them…and I can remember at times Dad as an adult showing me something and saying to me, 'Is that the way you'd word it?' So they never did have total confidence [in] their knowledge."

When she was a child in the 1930s, Marion Bell probably accepted her parents' social and economic place in the Buckingham community without question. However, she may also have absorbed Agnes's kindness. In the 1930s – during the Depression years – beggars often came to the door, and Agnes would feed them. Moreover, although Agnes never learned French and her husband knew the language, it appears that she was more sensitive to the discrimination the francophone majority suffered in Buckingham than Wilson Bell was. Ted Bell told me that his father never forgot the orphanage and consequently bore a grudge against francophones. He would, if they were lost on the road, ask for directions, "and he'd let the guy flounder, never letting on he could speak French. He was 'getting even.' My mother hated that."

Agnes and Wilson both had extended family in Canada. Wilson's sister Hilda and his two elder brothers, William and Berniad (or Bernard as he called himself in Canada as an adult) remained part of his life, and Wilson looked after his Aunt Ada, the one who had rescued him and Hilda from the orphanage.[21] In the 1920s and early 1930s, before they moved to Masson, the Bell's Montreal house was a duplex, and one of Wilson Bell's brothers lived in the adjacent apartment. The two families were close, and for Agnes those Bell relatives were "her support system."

But Gail Frith, Olive Bell's daughter, explained to me that it was Agnes's twin sisters, Nellie and Cissie, who were the dominant relatives. They each visited often, and when the Bells went on holiday the two sisters were always included. Both remained unmarried and they were devoted aunts to Agnes's children, bestowing love and concern on all three of them. For Marion they served as examples

The Bell family, on horseback.
Marion is on the left, and her
father Wilson Bell is on the right.
Ted and Olive are in the middle.
C. 1940.

of independent women who managed their lives successfully. They began their lives as "domestics" but, like Agnes and Wilson, they too raised their economic and social status. Nellie (Ellen) became a seamstress – a respectable and responsible job – at the St. James's Club on Dorchester Avenue in Montreal. Cissie (Bridget) worked for a rich family in Rockliffe Park, Ottawa's fanciest suburb. Many years later, Marion Dewar told Greta Hofmann Nemiroff that the two aunts lived together after they retired. Cissie dropped dead at ninety-seven: "She said to us she wasn't feeling well and sat down. My sister put her arm around her and said, 'Is there something wrong, Aunt Cissie?' And she said, 'Of course! I wouldn't be sitting here if there wasn't,' closed her eyes, and that was it!"

Given the effort that Agnes and Wilson put into raising their social status, it is remarkable that they also had the inclination and the energy to provide a lively and creative household for themselves and their three children. Marion would later say to Hofmann Nemiroff: "It was a very dynamic relationship. And I used to think they fought a lot. And I began to realize, they just communicated at a high level."

Marion and Ted both remembered their parents as avid readers. Discussion in the family was free, easy, and open. The household was also open to the children's friends. One such friend was Florence Stoodley Berndt, who met and became close friends with Marion when they were both twelve years old and in grade 8. "My name is Marion Bell, what's yours?" Florence remembers Marion saying, and they were friends from then on. Florence, who was from Thurso, a lumber town on the Ottawa River, went to school in Buckingham. During the week she boarded with a family and sometimes she spent the weekends in Buckingham, often with the Bells.

Florence told me a delightful story. She and Marion were fourteen at the time. Marion's sister Olive, by then twenty-one, had a date with a young man who was taking her to a formal dance. The two fourteen-year-old girls traipsed about after Olive as she dressed and prepared for the evening. When a florist brought Olive's corsage, Mrs. Bell allowed the two girls to look at it before she put it in the refrigerator to keep fresh. When Olive's date arrived, Marion and Florence peeped down the curved staircase to witness her departure. Florence also recalls that Mrs. Bell made delicious baked apples. She would bake them and leave them on the kitchen counter for the girls. At school recess, Florence and Marion would run home to the Bell house, eat the apples quickly, and then return to school. Florence remembers Agnes Bell as warm, welcoming, and always kind.

It appears that the Bell family adopted modern, upper-middle-class notions of parenthood. Both parents hoped their rise in social status and income would improve things for their children. They thought about their children's future, focused attention on them, and did everything they could to ensure their well-being. This applied to their education and to their health. Florence Berndt remembers that Marion had braces on her teeth, which was unusual in the 1940s, and that she wanted them too.

THE INFLUENCE OF GENDER AND RELIGION

But not everything was easy. There were complicated tensions concerning gender roles. Marion, the baby, appears to have been universally loved, and to have been unequivocally successful at home and in school. Her older sister, Olive, also had a forceful personality and a successful childhood. Much later, however, reflecting on the fact that her father refused to let her go to Queen's University to study science, Marion held that she and Olive had been short-changed because they were girls, and that Ted, the only boy, had been favoured. But Ted says that from his perspective it was the girls, and especially Marion, who were favoured, and that he could never satisfy his father. He was never smart enough for Wilson, and he never did well enough in school. He believes, however, that he was his mother's favourite child, and says of his mother and his father as parents, "They were known as gentle, kind, and loving people, and I do believe that Olive, Marion, and myself had the best parents on earth."

The Bells lived in a community that, although small, was complex. They themselves exemplified many of these complexities. They were part of the dominant English-speaking minority, and yet they were Catholic. However, they were unusual among anglophone Catholics because they were not Irish. And although Agnes and Wilson were both of working-class origin and had received only a limited formal education, they were self-educated to an unusual

The Bell family, 1942. Marion, Ted, and
Olive are standing. Wilson and Agnes Bell
are seated. Agnes's corsage and Wilson's and
Ted's buttonhole carnations suggest that
this was a special occasion.

degree. They were part of Buckingham's elite, and their children all received a thorough formal education as youngsters.

Catholicism was central to their lives. It was not until 1942 that there was an anglophone Catholic Church (Our Lady of Victory) in Buckingham, although anglophone Catholics had been working to establish such a congregation since the 1920s.[22] During the 1930s, the family's church was St.-Grégoire de Naziance, or St. Gregory's, as it was known in English. Marion Bell was deeply devout as a child. Norah Cassidy Renwick, who met Marion at elementary school, recalls an intense little girl. She was passionate about their friendship and told Norah that they must go to St.-Grégoire and swear to be friends for life, before God. Norah told her that they did not need to do that. "I said to her, but we are friends for life. We don't need the church. We'll be friends even if one of us lives in Timbuktu." But clearly Marion, as a small girl, was moved by the atmosphere of this big, handsome stone church, with its magnificent wooden pews, its stained glass windows, and hushed and sanctified air. It was here that she prayed each week, took her first communion, and experienced other landmarks in religious life.[23]

When it was time for Marion to go to school, she followed in her big sister Olive's footsteps and went to "the convent." This was the École St. Laurent, the parish primary school for girls, run by the Soeurs Grise (the Grey Nuns). The convent school was founded in 1869 and in the 1930s was still educating the Catholic girls of Buckingham and the surrounding region.[24] While French speakers were the majority among teachers and pupils, and dominated the school, it was bilingual. Norah Renwick recalled that there were six French classes and two English classes. It was, after all, the parish school, and the parish did contain a significant minority of anglophones. Marion was intelligent and outspoken as a child. "If you gave her a compliment she'd explode and roll on the floor," recalls Norah Renwick. "Other kids resented her because she was too smart."

Olive had been sent to the Rideau Street Convent in Ottawa for high school, leaving home at twelve to become a boarder there. Gail Frith said that her mother, Olive, hated the convent (she remembered bitterly that their exercise consisted of an occasional walk around the block), and likely because of her bad experience, Agnes and Wilson made another choice for their two younger children. They sent them both to Buckingham High School, breaking not with Catholicism but with Catholic education. Buckingham was an English-language school and also Protestant.

Buckingham High School, when Marion attended it, was housed in a small building on Church Street.[25] The school was coeducational, a new experience for Marion after the all-girls convent. Marion entered the school when she was twelve and attended for four years, graduating in 1944 when she was sixteen. That graduating class consisted of nine students: six girls and three boys. While there were more children in the lower grades, the numbers thinned out in the upper grades. Few families could afford to keep either their boys or their girls at school through grade 11, the final year of high school in Quebec.

The High School was collegiate in its curriculum and perfect for the studious, hard-working Marion. She excelled there, learning science, math, and history. Even in the 1990s she retained warm memories of the principal, Wayne Wendell Roberts, and of his thoughtful history lessons. She developed a love for science, which was encouraged by R.B. Walker, a chemical engineer who was the general manager at the Electric Reduction Corporation. Walker, who was a mentor to her, wanted her to go to university to do mathematics and physics, and she worked one summer in an ERCO laboratory.[26]

There was fun as well as work to be had in this environment of young girls and boys. One of my informants, Bruce Laforce, who knew Marion Bell during the two years that they were at Buckingham High School together, remembers that she came to the dances arranged by his crowd of young people. There was no gymnasium at the small Church Street school, so the boys and girls would have dances at their parents' houses. The youngsters and the parents would "make sandwiches, roll up the rugs, and dance till 2 a.m." But they were a "nice" group. They did not drink alcohol. One of the mothers played the piano, but most of the music came from records played on a record player.

Fifty years later, Marion recalled that she did have an "adolescent romance" at Buckingham High School. She dated a boy who would later become the organist at the United Church. "The parish priest

The graduating class, Buckingham High School, 1944. Marion Bell, who was 16, stands at the left. All but one of the graduating girls became nurses.

came down to see my mother...I shouldn't go with a Protestant [he said]. And my mother said that she would decide who was right and who was wrong for us. That there was lots of Catholics that she wouldn't like to see me going with."[27] But in fact, Agnes did want her children to marry Catholics, although when Olive married a Protestant, Gail Frith says she exhibited the same sort of tolerance. "Is he a nice man?" she asked Olive. "That's what matters." Kenneth Kimmerly agreed to raise the children Catholic, and he and Olive Bell were married at Our Lady of Victory Church in Buckingham in 1955.

Armed with her good grades and her successful experience at Buckingham High School, Marion was sent to Ottawa to take Ontario's grade 13. She lived with her Aunt Nellie and went to Nepean High for the first semester, but she completed her year at Glebe Collegiate Institute, doing well and gaining admission with a scholarship to Queen's University to study science. And then she met with the first serious barrier of her life. Her father refused to let her go to Queen's. "'No daughter of mine is going to take a course like that. Your brother is going to university and wants to take engineering and that's proper....Take something like teaching or nursing. That would be fine,' my dad said."[28]

Why didn't her mother stand up for her? Olive, Ted, and Marion had been brought up to be confident and to value and employ their intelligence. Agnes and Wilson did want the best for their children. Marion's niece Gail Frith told me that her Aunt Marion said of Agnes that "deep down she was a feminist." This was wishful thinking. Agnes was intelligent and tough-minded, and she could be blunt and outspoken, but she was no feminist. She did not work outside the home, devoting herself instead to the children, the house, and her husband, and Wilson was the dominant figure. Marion was "the baby" and most likely Wilson's favourite, and he valued how smart she was. "Ask the baby," he would say if anyone else in the family had an unsolved problem. But still, at this crucial moment, he insisted that she adopt a set of prescribed gender roles. She might be the apple of his eye, the "spoiled" daughter to be pro-tected from hard knocks, but he prevented her from doing what she most wanted to do.

Marion could have rebelled at this juncture and fled her family. But she did no such thing. Instead, she returned to Buckingham after her graduation from Glebe Collegiate. She may have been indignant, but still she went home. She lived with her parents and worked at the Bank of Nova Scotia. She hated the bank and she was bored and restless. She decided she would go to nursing school, even though she would be giving in to her father's wishes. Her older sister Olive had paved the way, graduating with an RN diploma from the Ottawa General Hospital's School of Nursing, and then going on to McGill to receive a bachelor's degree in public health in 1944, the same year Marion graduated from Buckingham High School.[29]

In 1946 Marion did look into the Ottawa General Hospital's School of Nursing. As she recalled years later, "I went in and I met a nun who was supervisor who said 'You're Miss Bell's sister…. Oh, she was such a good student! And she was so wonderful.'" Marion went home afterward and told her mother, "I'm not going to the General. I'm not going anywhere as anybody's sister."[30] Agnes understood. She told Marion that she could go wherever she wanted for her nursing training, as long as she chose a Catholic school.

There is plenty of evidence that there was competition and even conflict between Olive and Marion throughout their lives. When Marion was in her mid-teens, her good friend Florence Berndt remembers that at one point Olive was at home – perhaps on a break from her public health studies at McGill – and Agnes did not make her do the dishes, but Marion had to do them: "Who does she think she is," said Marion, "the Duchess of Windsor?" Marion Dewar's daughters Liz and Cathy and their cousin Gail all remember closeness, but also competition and friction between their mother and Olive in later years.

Bob Dewar emphasized in one of his comments to me that the conflicts and the arguing involved all three of the Bells – Ted as well as Olive and Marion. Their favourite subjects were politics and the church or the details of their childhood. They loved each other and they were close, but loud, free, and fierce discussion was a major way in which they expressed their attachments to one another. Bob remembers one occasion at the Dewar cottage at Sand Point on the Ottawa River when everyone else drifted off and

Olive, Ted, and Marion were left talking, laughing, and arguing well into the night.

The nursing school Marion chose was in Kingston, the home of Queen's University, to which her father had not allowed her to go. It was the St. Joseph's School of Nursing, a three-year hospital-based school that awarded a registered nurse's diploma. (There were baccalaureate nursing programs in Canada; the first was established at the University of British Columbia in 1919. But until the late twentieth century, only a "small percentage" of Canadian nurses took a university degree in nursing.[31]) The school was attached to Kingston's Hotel Dieu Hospital. This remarkable English-speaking Catholic hospital had been founded by the Religious Hospitallers of St. Joseph, the order of nuns responsible for the Hotel Dieu in Montreal. The Montreal hospital's founder was Jeanne Mance, the redoubtable seventeenth-century French laywoman who came out to the New World and became "the first lay nurse in North America." The hospital, known in Kingston as "the Dieu" (pronounced "Dew"), is, says its historian, "the church in action."[32]

The hospital, which fought typhus, housed orphans, and cared for the poor, established its nursing school in 1912, when it became evident that the sisters could not singlehandedly do the work. North American hospital-based schools of nursing were often founded because the work of the student nurses was needed. As Canadian nursing historian Kathryn McPherson puts it, "The apprenticeship system [the three-year hospital-based training program] offered Canadian hospitals a number of advantages. The first was volume. Institutions could meet increased patient demand simply by accepting greater numbers of students."[33]

By the time Marion arrived, Kingston's Hotel Dieu school had been functioning for more than thirty years. She entered in 1946 and graduated in 1949, along with thirty-eight other young women. Only one was a member of a religious order, and all except one were Catholics. Most came from Ontario towns and cities, but some were from Quebec, including Marion and her friend Roberta Bisson, who was also from Buckingham.[34]

Although it had not been her first choice, she fell in love with nursing at St. Joseph's, and with good reason. It was a fine nursing school affiliated with an excellent hospital. Moreover, the school maintained high standards for admission. The young women admitted (there were no men) had to have achieved high standards in school and be "of outstanding moral character." They were seen as worthy and dedicated, and their work was valued. [35]

During the school's early years, the students had learned nursing "at the bedside."[36] By the 1940s St. Joseph's had adopted a mixture of classes and ward work. In 1946, the year Marion Bell entered, the school introduced the "Block" system, which comprised alternating blocks of classes with ward work. The students began their first year with classes, which were taught by physicians, nursing sisters, nurses, and priests. In the first year, two hundred hours were devoted to "Principles and Practice of Nursing Including Hospital Housekeeping, Massage, Bandaging, and Charting." Twenty-four hours were devoted to "Nursing Ethics." During Marion Bell's time as a student nurse, the ethics course was taught by the chaplain, the Reverend Father Sullivan.[37]

Many of the students were housed at St. Mary's of the Lake Hospital. They commuted back and forth "by the legendary 'Black Maria' driven by Tim Downey."[38] Their day began early in the morning, and before they boarded the "Black Maria" – slang for police van – they had to get dressed in their uniforms. Historian Christina Bates, in her book *A Cultural History of the Nurse's Uniform*, has much to say about the uniforms worn by nursing students. The uniforms were to be attractive and "feminine": after all, Bates comments, most of these young women would marry, and most would never practise as graduate nurses. The uniform St. Joseph's students wore in Marion Bell's day was not as confining as earlier versions, but it was still stiff, starched, and complicated. It was "a short-sleeved blue shirt dress with white collar and cuffs." Over this, the probationers wore a "white apron."[39]

The nursing school program was gruelling. The students worked twelve-hour days. But it was also rewarding, according to several of my informants who were students at the school at the time. They all said that although it was tough, they were learning, they always felt supported by the nuns and by the physicians, and they really got to know and help their patients. Bernadette Cotman told me, "It was hard, but you were learning all the time." I asked if it was too hard. "We never really thought anything about it. People

treated you very well." Elizabeth Lowden said, "The young women who came for training had self-discipline…. We just knew what we could do…. We enjoyed our work."

A capping ceremony at St. Joseph's School of Nursing. Archivist Rodney Carter pointed out to me that this is a pre-Vatican II photograph. The priest is facing the altar, not the congregation.

In April 2012, when I visited the St. Joseph's School of Nursing archives, I was invited to lunch. I sat with Sister Loretta Gaffney and Sister Aurora Beaulieu. Both said that they had received excellent training at the school.

St. Joseph's was very much a Catholic school. The hospital chaplain was involved in teaching Nursing Ethics, and daily Mass was part of the routine. At the end of their first four months, just before Christmas, the probationers – wearing their blue uniforms and stiffly starched white aprons – received their caps from the chaplain in a solemn religious ceremony. At the "capping" ceremony, the priest placed the caps on the students. In a photograph of the ceremony, we see the probationers assembled downstairs in the chapel and the nuns upstairs. The young nurses go to the altar and kneel, and the priest puts on the cap.[40]

Although they were closely monitored, with curfews and rules about their behaviour, the young women did have fun. Marion was well respected and popular with the staff and the other students. One of my interviewees told me a story. At the eighteen-month point in their training (halfway through the program) my informant and

Marion went out to dinner to celebrate at a restaurant on Kingston's Brock Street. They were having a good time and laughing a lot. Well, it appears that there was a spy there, who reported to the sisters that my informant (Bernadette Cotman) had been drinking. As Mrs. Cotman explained, some 65 years later, she had certainly not been drinking. She had taken a pledge in high school that she would not drink alcohol until she was twenty-one, and there was no way she would break that pledge. She was called into the Mother Superior's office and accused of drinking. She felt helpless. But when Marion found out, she stormed into the Mother Superior's office herself and told her that there was no way her friend could have been drinking. That did the trick. "I could have been expelled," she remembered. Instead, she went on to have a long and distinguished career at the Hotel Dieu Hospital.

SETTING OUT ON HER VOCATION

Marion graduated, along with her thirty-eight classmates, on Wednesday June 1, 1949, at a ceremony held in Grant Hall, at Queen's University. Marion was one of the award winners. She received a General Proficiency Medal and the Religious Hospitallers Award, presented to her by the chaplain, Father Sullivan. The graduating nurses recited the Jeanne Mance Pledge, which begins, "That I may be strengthened in my resolve to model my life of duty after that of Jeanne Mance, the first lay nurse of my beloved Canada.... I will be true to the practice of religion, which is the inspiration of my noble vocation...." The popular and active Father Sullivan had written this pledge – with its Canadian and Catholic references – especially for St. Joseph's in 1943.[41] Previously, the graduating nurses had recited the Florence Nightingale Pledge, used at most North American schools of nursing.[42] The Nightingale Pledge, like the Jeanne Mance Pledge, stressed that nursing was to be seen as a vocation rather than as mere paid labour.

But times were changing. Marion's class of 1949, as a story in the *Kingston Whig Standard* attests, was the first to graduate in white mortarboards and gowns, which the young nurses wore over their uniforms. In his address to the students and their families, Mayor Curtin of Kingston talked about a "new spirit in nursing." Nursing was becoming a profession as well as a vocation.[43]

In November 1949, Marion Bell took and passed the Registered Nurses Association of Ontario qualifying examination. She was ready to begin her career as a nurse. In 1949 she wanted to nurse, but she also wanted adventure. She and her good friend and fellow St. Joseph's graduate Mary Jane McGonnigal (who would later marry Marion's brother Ted Bell) moved to Ottawa together. There they believed they would be well positioned to take any promising job offers that might arise, whether they were in the United States or Canada.

The graduating class, St. Joseph's School of Nursing, Hotel Dieu Hospital, Kingston, Ontario. Prizewinner Marion Bell is seated in the front row. She's the 5th student from the left.

Marion got a job at the Ottawa Civic Hospital. There she would meet Kenneth Dewar, her future husband and the love of her life. "I met him, I had him as a patient. He was twenty-eight. And he had a massive thrombosis. And they didn't think he was going to live. I was very attracted to him...."[44] Ken, born in 1923, was an Ottawa man from a Catholic family. He had attended Ottawa's English-Catholic St. Patrick's High School and had then served in the military during the Second World War. When he returned home, he got a job as a federal public servant, working in the customs branch. Marion's daughter Liz, who would become a nurse herself, would tease her mother about meeting their father in hospital. "I told her that she would have been in trouble with the College of Nurses for going with a patient." But her mother replied indignantly, "I didn't date him till after; [when] he wasn't my patient."

Marion and Mary Jane had rented an apartment together, and when Ken was discharged from the Civic Hospital, "he used to come up and visit and that's when we started going together." They did "fall madly in love"[45] and quickly got engaged. In the months before their marriage, they had an enjoyable, lively courtship that included outings to the Chateau Laurier Hotel, then Ottawa's most elegant location.

Marion said, "When I first began to date Ken, we went to the Canadian Grill at the Chateau Laurier quite often. I can recall the charm of the place...our dates there were always special."[46] For such an outing Marion would most likely have worn a dressy dress, with a calf-length full skirt, in the New Look fashion of the 1940s and 1950s, and Ken would have worn a suit and tie.

Marion and Mary Jane's apartment in downtown Ottawa was only a few blocks from the Dewar home, where twenty-eight-year-old Ken was living. Marion's mother, Agnes, decided that once the two were engaged this proximity was inappropriate. So twenty-two-year-old Marion dutifully went back to the family home in Buckingham.

She took a job as a nurse at L'Hôpital St-Michel de Buckingham, known in English simply as the Buckingham Hospital. Founded in 1906, it was a Catholic hospital when Marion Bell worked there, managed by the Grey Nuns. But it took in English as well as French patients, Protestants as well as Catholics, and there were English-speaking Protestant nurses and physicians on the staff. Florence Stoodley Berndt worked there as a nurse for many years. She had trained at the Ottawa Civic Hospital and later did a postgraduate year at the Boston Lying-In Hospital in Boston, Massachusetts. Florence Berndt was English-speaking and Protestant, although she knew some French. She got along well at Buckingham Hospital, though she remained an outsider. Florence recounted one incident that reveals both her outsider status as a Protestant and her insider status as a good friend and a fellow nurse:

Sister Paul Eugene! A good nurse, she had a sense of humour like mine…. The two of us were at the nurses' station one time when a priest, holding up something sacred, chanting, was leading an entourage down the hospital corridor to a small shrine. At the desk was a music box, sculpted figures depicting a praying Mary and kneeling children. As the group – Immaculate Conception Day, I think – neared us, that box began to play!!! And loud!! The Sister Superior, in the procession, looked at us, horrified, while Sister Paul Eugene frantically pushed the off button. It would not stop! She shoved it at me. "Here," she hissed, "put your heretic hands on it, that'll stop it!"[47]

Buckingham Hospital proved to be a challenging experience for Marion Bell. First of all, she had to acquire some knowledge of French. Second, Marion was shocked and appalled to find that the hospital's doctors were in some cases performing abortions, and not infrequently late-term abortions. Marion, who would later become a champion of contraception and would even advocate "a woman's right to choose," was still very much opposed to abortion as a nurse and as a devout Catholic in the early 1950s. Moreover, she objected to the way that doctors at the hospital were openly flouting the law, and she spoke out against them within the hospital setting. Florence Berndt remembers how shocked Marion was by the abortions. And as Marion herself recalled years later, "When I was twenty-one, twenty-two, I was in the Buckingham Hospital. They were breaking the law, they were doing abortions right, left, and centre…very late. And they were doing them because there was no prenatal care. And the doctors were having a ball making all sorts of money [this was before the Canada Health Act, and patients had to pay, if they could]…and abortions, at that point, I thought, were terrible."

She was a young and inexperienced nurse. It took bravery and a social conscience for her to speak out. Yes, she was "madly in love" with Ken, but this did not lessen her sense of commitment to wider issues and to her community.[48]

ENDNOTES:

[10] See baptismal record, Holy Family Church B15 for 1928.

[11] I thank historian Denyse Baillargeon, professor of history at the Université de Montréal, for discussing Montreal orphanages with me.

[12] For Wilson Bell's occupations, see Wilson Edward Bell's (Ted's) baptismal record from St. Michael the Archangel Church, on Saint-Viateur St., in Montreal, which states his occupation as "Chauffeur." Genealogist and family historian Bruce Murduck found this and a number of other salient records that I mention below, including the City Directory entries for Wilson Bell listing him in the Lovell's Montreal [1928] Alphabetical Directory as an electrician.

[13] For Agnes Bell's place of birth as Coatbridge, Scotland, in Landing Records, Canadian Government Return: Canadian Immigration Service, Agnes Bell, children Olive, Teddy, Marion, and the aunts: They sailed on the *Letitia*, from Glasgow to Quebec, arriving 8/3/1929; vol. 17, 76.

[14] Agnes and Bridget returned together on the *Cassandra*, sailing from Glasgow to Quebec: pg 3, lines 1 and 2, RG 76, T-14703.

[15] St. Dominic's Parish records, M [marriage] 18 for 1920.

[16] See Munro and Medelko; Lapointe (2006, 1990); Threlfall; for interesting discussions of Buckingham, the surrounding area, and its industries at this time. See also the 1999 TV series *Sketches of our Town*, which included one of Buckingham, Quebec, http://locatetv.com/tv/sketches-of-our-town/1327429; and the film *Morning on the Lièvre*, 1961, David Bairstow producer, National Film Board of Canada: http://nfb.ca/film/morning_on_the_lièvre, accessed June 4, 2016.

[17] "Grand Dieu, ils tirent pour tuer…" in Pierre-Louis Lapointe, *Buckingham: ville occupée* (Gatineau, QC: Les editions Asticou enrg., 1983), 71.

[18] See Lapointe (2006), 224–226, for "La Liste Noire."

[19] Munro & Medelko, 15; also Lapointe (1990), 236–237.

[20] Leonore Davidoff, *The Best Circles: Society, Etiquette and the Season* (London: Croom Helm, 1973). Davidoff is discussing a different country, century, and social class. Nonetheless, she succeeds admirably in depicting women's crucial role in changing a family's social status.

[21] Lovell's Montreal Alphabetical Directory, 1927. For Berniad, who became "Bernard," see Montreal Directory, 1919, p. 761: "Bell, Bernard, window decorator 432 First Ave, Hochelaga ward." "Miss Ada Bell" is in 1927 at 5501 St. Michel Rd., Montreal. [Bernard is at 5503 St. Michel Rd. on the same page.]

[22] I am so grateful to Bill and Linda Cameron, of Buckingham, who gave me information about the church, of which they are members. See also Lapointe (1990), 306–313.

[23] Celine of the Paroisse Saint Grégoire (email: 2/13/2012): "I found the date for the confirmation, not the First Communion for Marion Hilda Bell: October 2, 1935."

[24] See Commission Scolaire au Coeur-des-Vallées: "École St-Laurent de Buckingham: 130 ans d'histoire 1869-1999" stamped "Soeurs de la Charité d'Ottawa, Maison Mère Archives."

[25] Dick Clark, *History of Buckingham High School* (Courtesy of Allan Todd).

[26] Hofmann Nemiroff interview.

[27] Ibid.

[28] Marion Dewar told this story often. See Norma McCabe, "Setting the Pace at City Hall: Ottawa Mayor Marion Dewar is a product of on-the-job training," *Globe and Mail*, January 14, 1984, L5.

[29] From the yearbook "Old McGill 1944" sent to me by Krista Jamieson of Graduate Studies, Nursing, McGill University. Entry for Olive Bell, RN: "Born June 11 1921 at Montreal, Quebec. Received high school education at Rideau Convent Ottawa. Graduated from University of Ottawa School of Nursing 1941. Worked with Victorian Order of Nurses in Chatham, ON, for one and a half years. Enrolled in PH nursing school at McGill, Sept 1941."

[30] Hofmann Nemiroff interview.

[31] Kathryn M. McPherson, *Bedside Matters: The Transformation of Canadian Nursing, 1900-1990* (Toronto and New York: Oxford University Press, 1996), 31. For the U.S., see Malka, 20–21.

[32] Jessie V. Deslauriers, *Hotel Dieu Hospital Kingston, 1845-1995* (Kingston, ON: Hotel Dieu Hospital, 1995); for the "church in action," I; for Jeanne Mance, 3.

[33] McPherson, 27 and passim.

[34] "St Joseph's School of Nursing Hotel Dieu Hospital Graduation Exercises, Wednesday, June 1, 1949, Grant Hall Queen's University." I thank archivist Rodney Carter for this and much more. It was Carter who told me that one of the women in the class of 1949 was Protestant. When I visited in 2012 Rodney Carter was archivist of the St. Joseph Region Archives, Religious Hospitallers of St. Joseph (RHSJ), then located at 16 Manitou Crescent East, Kingston, ON, K7N 1B2. It was home to some of the few remaining Sisters of the RHSJ and also to the archives of the St. Joseph's School of Nursing. Rodney Carter remains archivist, but the archives are now at the Hotel Dieu Hospital in Kingston.

[35] See Deslauriers, 154, for admission standards. See also *St Josephs School of Nursing Calendar, 1947-8, Hotel Dieu Hospital*.

[36] Deslauriers, 27.

[37] See typescript "Curriculum 1945–1946" from "St Joseph's School of

Nursing, Hotel Dieu Hospital, Kingston, Report of the Intermediate Block and Curriculum Outlines" 84, 6/158.

[38] Deslauriers, 154.

[39] Christina Bates, *A Cultural History of the Nurse's Uniform* (Gatineau, QC: Canadian Museum of Civilization, 2012), 30 and following. For the modifications of the 1940s, see Deslauriers, 157–159.

[40] McPherson, 30. In the mid-twentieth century, capping ceremonies were common in all Canadian hospital-based schools.

[41] Deslauriers, 151.

[42] Dr. Susan Gelfand Malka, personal communication. The Nightingale Pledge does mention "God" but in a brief and general way.

[43] City of Ottawa Archives, Marion Dewar Fonds, 2010-076, Box 1 1988-2002. Clipping from *Kingston Whig Standard* June 2, 1949, 15. The story mentions that "Marion H. Bell of Buckingham," who sat in the front row, was "one of four medalists."

[44] Hofmann Nemiroff interview.

[45] Ibid.

[46] Joan Rankin, *Meet Me at the Chateau; A Legacy of Memory* (Toronto: Heritage Books, 1990), 165. Marion recalled this fondly while Rankin was preparing her book.

[47] Florence Berndt's memories. See Lapointe (1990), 271-278 for the hospital.

[48] Hofmann Nemiroff interview. This was the late 1940s, well before the Criminal Law Amendment Act of 1968. Abortions of the kind Marion Bell Dewar described were definitely illegal.

Chapter 2
A SUBURBAN HOUSEWIFE?

Marion Bell and Ken Dewar were married in Buckingham at Our Lady of Victory Church on September 15, 1951. Marion was the first of the Bell children to marry, and her mother was determined that the event would be worthy of the family's hard-won high status in the community. Florence Stoodley Berndt mentions that Agnes hosted a "lovely trousseau tea," an event held close to the wedding date where the wedding gifts were displayed. The tea itself was for women only but, as Florence recalls, Marion's brother Ted was there in the kitchen, "kidding with a pretty French girl that Mrs. Bell had hired to help."

The wedding was described at length in a two-column story in the *Buckingham Post*.[49] It was "a very pretty wedding," wrote the reporter. Marion was "given away by her father.... For her wedding, the attractive young bride wore a floor length gown of white chiffon French velvet made on simple lines with a long torso effect..." The gown had a train, and the bride wore a "fingertip veil of tulle illusion." Agnes wore blue and Ken's mother wore brown. Olive Bell and Mary Jane McGonnigal were attendants and Ted was an usher. After a reception in the Legion Hall, the couple left on their wedding trip, a motor tour through northern New York State, the Muskoka region, and Algonquin Park.

From the vantage point of the twenty-first century, we may well ask: Did Marion want this conventional wedding? Or did she subject herself to these rituals – being "given away," for example

A wedding photograph of Marion and Ken at their reception in the Legion Hall, Buckingham, Quebec, September 15, 1951. The ceremony took place at Our Lady of Victory Church, Buckingham's English-Catholic Church. The photo includes Marion's two bridesmaids, her sister Olive and Mary Jane McGonnigal. On the right is Marion's brother Ted.

– for the sake of her family? After all, she had already demonstrated that she was a strong person with passionate beliefs who was brave enough to defend them even in the face of hostility.

But this was 1951, and Marion was only twenty-three. Her intelligence, compassion, and courage were already evident, but she was also very much the beloved youngest daughter, her father's favourite child. She was also still a traditional Catholic. And while she must have known that her mother's love for her was the primary reason for the display that accompanied her wedding, she surely also knew that a secondary reason was that this public occasion both reflected and enhanced the Bells' social standing in the Buckingham community.

BEGINNING A FAMILY IN OTTAWA:
CHALLENGES AND SUCCESSES

After the wedding and the motor trip, Marion and Ken settled down to married life in Ottawa. They were living in a downtown apartment, at 2 Driveway, near the Cartier Square Drill Hall. Bob Dewar remembers seeing the Changing of the Guard marshalling there when he was a small boy. Marion got pregnant almost right away, and in June 1952 she gave birth to Bob, who was sickly as a newborn. That was difficult, but even more difficult was the fact that Marion quickly discovered that Ken had a serious drinking problem. He thought he had put it behind him, but it re-emerged with Marion's pregnancy.

Marion recalled to Hofmann Nemiroff that she decided where to go for help herself, without anyone's support. She was resourceful and she was a nurse. She telephoned Alcoholics Anonymous (AA), then a relatively new organization (it had been founded in 1935), and told the person who answered, "I think I've got a problem."[50] What were the implications of Marion Dewar's decision to contact AA? By contacting AA for herself and for Ken, she transformed Ken from a man who got drunk when his wife was having a baby into an alcoholic, and she transformed herself into the wife of an alcoholic.

Marion Dewar probably made a wise choice when she telephoned AA. As Bette Tallen puts it, "Much is quite admirable about Alcoholics Anonymous, its offshoot organizations, and the Twelve Steps themselves…. It has literally saved the lives of thousands of men and women who otherwise would have died because of their drinking."[51] Tallen is a feminist critic of AA, so it is especially significant that she supports it. However, there is no question that Alcoholics Anonymous imposes a formulaic definition upon its adherents. The "problem drinker" becomes "the alcoholic self."[52]

Alcoholics Anonymous held then and still holds that drinkers with problems have an illness and must strive to achieve "sobriety," abstaining altogether and forever from alcohol. AA was and is a self-help group, organized by and for alcoholics. No experts are involved. Although it took Ken several years to see his drinking as a serious problem, and at first he would have nothing to do with AA, Marion did go to Al-Anon meetings and found them not only helpful but transformative. Bob Dewar remembers how important Al-Anon was to his mother. Discussing her Al-Anon involvement of the 1950s with Greta Hofmann Nemiroff in the 1990s, Marion Dewar said that her Al-Anon meetings helped her to force Ken to take responsibility for his drinking. "I refused to make decisions for him…and part of that became part of my…strong feminist socializing…."

A wedding photograph of Marion
with Mary Jane McGonnigal, who
would soon marry Marion's brother
Ted. September 15, 1951.

Al-Anon was organized in 1951 by two American wives of alcoholics. One of them was Lois Wilson, the wife of Bill Wilson, one of the two founders of AA. The great majority (about 80–85 per cent) of those who go to Al-Anon meetings are women, and in North America, they are predominantly white and from the middle class. Al-Anon, like AA, is a twelve-step program, and there are many references in the Twelve Steps to God and to the importance of spirituality. The emphasis on belief was and is off-putting for many problem drinkers and their family members, but it would not have been a problem for either Marion or Ken Dewar, who were both devout Catholics. Marion would have liked the Al-Anon message that she did not cause Ken's drinking, that she could not control it, and that she could not cure it. She took from that message the idea that she needed to live her own independent life, in spite of being married to an alcoholic.

She was certainly not the only woman to gain strength from Al-Anon, as research on this subject bears out. There is, for example, the interesting participant-observation research done by Grazyna Zajdow, an Australian of Polish origin. Although she began to go to Al-Anon meetings with "skepticism and distrust," in the end she notes that there were some "warm and inviting women who made me feel welcome, and slowly I began to feel that the part of my life which had brought me to this point was becoming easier to bear."[53]

We have no way of knowing what Marion Dewar's Ottawa Al-Anon meetings of the 1950s were like. We do know that AA, as opposed to Al-Anon, was and remains a very male organization, and it and its affiliate groups did not and do not now challenge conventional beliefs about the family or conventional gender roles. Moreover, as feminist analysts have pointed out, there is now a "recovery" industry, which has grown in recent decades into unthinking advocacy of the concept of "co-dependency" as a "disease."[54]

Pathology was the model for psychiatrists, psychologists, and social workers in the 1950s as well. Wives of alcoholics were then labelled as "enablers" and as neurotic women who needed to "control" men.[55] The fact that Dewar did not label herself an enabler or, worse yet, in later years, a co-dependent, suggests that the stereotype of the enabler wife who thrives on her husband's alcoholism is just that – a stereotype. Both Marion and Ken avoided these labels.

They took what they needed from Al-Anon and A A. Marion Dewar constructed her own very successful public life, and Ken – "the perfect political wife," as one of my respondents called him – was supportive of her and, moreover, used A A to help himself remain sober most of the time.

By the winter of 1951–1952, Marion had the support of her mother. Agnes turned up at the door one day unannounced: "I was in a dressing gown. Beside myself, I was sick, and my marriage was on the rocks." Her mother asked her what was wrong. "And I burst into tears of course…'[Ken's] drinking.'" "Oh, my God! You've got an alcoholic on your hands…." said her mother. "Well, for God's sake, go and get dressed and put some make-up on. I'd drink too if I came home to that!"[56]

Agnes's reaction may seem old-fashioned and even sexist in its assumptions about the role of a wife, but it helped her daughter. It was of immense value to Marion that Agnes could look the problem squarely in the face without denying it. Moreover, Agnes realized that Marion needed to work, even if it was for only one day a week. "Why don't you go and use that R N you have….?" Agnes said.

Marion later said of her mother: "My, she was so wise! She had no education and she was so wise…and she knew that my self-confidence was more important than anything else. She always understood that."

Marion began working one shift a week at the Ottawa Civic Hospital, usually at night, even when Bob was a baby. "It kept me in contact with my sister nurses. And also with the adult world. And that life was mine…. The expression used at home at that time was…it was Mommy's night out. When I went to the hospital, I was me. I wasn't the mother of or the wife of."[57]

Bob Dewar told me that when his mother was in hospital giving birth to him, his father was drunk. Agnes told Ken he'd better sober up: he now had lots of responsibilities. And for decades he did, which showed enormous strength of character and will. But Ken began drinking again in 1978, when Marion was running for mayor and Wilson Bell (Marion's father) was dying. Ken had trouble with alcohol in the late 1970s and 1980s, his "darkest period," but for the last decade of his life he was sober.

I asked Bob how his mother coped: "She joined Al-Anon. She

would get angry at Ken. She would sometimes say, 'Leave until you sober up.'" Ken did go to rehabilitation programs, once at Homewood in Guelph, Ontario, and once in Massachusetts. Bob says that after his initial reluctance, his father was a longtime AA member. He went to meetings regularly and served as a sponsor. (An AA sponsor is an AA member who has managed to remain sober and who takes on responsibility for a newer, more vulnerable member.) Paul Dewar believes that his father's drinking problems had their origin in his wartime experiences.

From 1952 to 1963, Marion and Ken had four children: Robert (Bob) in 1952, Elizabeth (Liz) in 1956, Catherine (Cathy) in 1960, and Paul in 1963. For the first few years, they continued to live at 2 Driveway. In 1956, the year of Liz Dewar's birth and of Agnes Bell's death, they moved to the modest house on Rex Avenue in Ottawa's west end, where they would live for the rest of their lives.

They established a household that was lively and open, encouraging their children and others who might be living with them to discuss almost all topics with intensity, including politics, religion, and books. (Sex seems to have been the exception. Cathy Dewar recalls that she could talk more easily to her big sister, Liz, than to her mother about getting her first period.) These discussions took place most often at the dinner table, in a family for which a shared dinner was a family affair. In fostering such free and open dialogue, Paul Dewar told me, Marion and Ken were building on the traditions of the Bell family rather than those of the Dewars, who were not open in this or other ways.

Proud new mother with infant Bob, the first child. 1952.

Marion and Ken with Bob and
newborn Liz. January, 1959.

As small children the four Dewars played
with each other and with children in the neighbourhood, which in the 1950s and 1960s was
more rural than suburban. For example, they would play "church," a
common game in Catholic households. (One Catholic respondent,
Philip Goldring, told me that this game, called Mass in his family,
was a "great excuse to light candles.") Bob, who was an altar boy in
everyday life, would always get to be the priest. As Paul remembered
it to me, "Bob was a very strict padre...."

All four of Marion and Ken's children had a happy and relatively
carefree childhood. Bob says of his mother, "She told you, you could
do anything you put your mind to. She was a very positive person."
He also remembers their frugal style of life. To save money, they
used powdered milk. Bob thought everyone's milk had little lumps
in it. Bob also remembers enjoying the Dewar family cottage at
Sand Point.

Liz still has fond memories of her Grandfather Bell. When Liz
was four, Wilson was a widower, living with Agnes' older sister

Nellie in a company house in Buckingham. He would come to Marion and Ken's every Friday afternoon and stay for dinner. On these days, he would wake up little Liz after her nap. She was always a bit grumpy after her nap, she says, but Grandfather Bell would cheer her up.

Their third child, Cathy, was ten when she went to camp in the summer of 1970. "I am home-sick for you all," she wrote, and she asked for information about the family garden. But she was having fun at Camp Tekakwitha, a Catholic girls' camp at Barry's Bay, Ontario. The lively and happy girl she was then shines through in her comments: "We changed our cabin into an undersea world," she told her family. And she enjoyed a folk Mass. "Please right [sic]," she said.[58]

A family photograph, circa 1968. Ken Dewar is in the background. In the foreground are Paul, Cathy, Marion, and Liz.

Paul, the youngest child, has the happiest as well as the clearest memories of his childhood. "It was a supportive and loving atmosphere," he recollects. It was also a busy household: "We were very different from some other families because Mum and Dad were so active in social action through the church."

When Paul started school, however, he and his family had to confront a serious problem. Paul was severely dyslexic. When he was eight and in grade 3, he still could not read. His parents did everything they could to help him. They read to him, they talked to him all the time and he listened to the CBC. He was placed in a special class for a while, but that was not a great experience, and in any case it was short-lived. For most of his elementary school years he went to St. Basil's, the local Catholic school. That was, he says, a "lesson in stigmatization."

Although all four of the Dewar children were happy when they were young, for the three older children adolescence proved to be stormy and difficult. Bob ran into serious trouble when he reached his teens. He experimented with drugs, had difficulties at school, and clashed with his parents.[59] (It was Bob who experienced the upheaval and chaos of the 1960s. Marion experienced such problems indirectly, through her volunteer work with young drug addicts.)

Liz followed her mother and her Aunt Olive (with whom she was close) into nursing, but she remembers that her life did change for the worse in 1972, when she was sixteen and her mother began her public career. Liz has positive memories of Marion and Ken's commitment to open discussion and democratic values. However, when she reached her teens, she began to realize that at times they honoured this commitment more in theory than in practice. At a family council meeting, for example, she remembers being asked if she wanted a young girl who needed a refuge to come and live at Rex Avenue:

"Do you want X to come and live here?"

"No," Liz said.

But her No was simply ignored.

"Well, X will have Liz's bedroom..." said her mother.

Liz and Cathy had difficulties in part because they were girls and had to deal with their mother's unacknowledged ambivalence about gender roles. I asked each of the Dewar children whether it was easier to be Bob or Paul than to be Liz or Cathy. All agreed that the boys had an easier time of it. Marion Dewar was an advocate for women even in the 1960s and 1970s, but she was still primarily a traditional wife and mother, and she experienced considerable guilt and anxiety about her house and family when she became a public figure. Her daughter Liz told me that her mother would become frustrated because their "home wasn't clean enough." Bob recalls that the Dewars did occasionally hire household help but never on a regular basis. She did expect the girls to take on traditionally female tasks. Cathy remembers that when Liz left home, "I was expected to make meals." She was then in grade 11. Cathy and her mother clashed, and Cathy left home when she was seventeen and moved into an apartment with Alderman Toddy Kehoe's daughter. Cathy worked at The Old Spaghetti Factory, a large restaurant chain that at the time had an Ottawa branch. For a while she did not speak to either of her parents.

Only Paul had a relatively untroubled adolescence. He largely credits this to the fact that his parents sought out and found a school for boys with learning disabilities that could help him. It was the Gow School, in upstate New York, which he attended during his last three years of high school. Although it was hard on his parents, and most especially on his mother, to have him leave home so early, Gow was "an entirely positive experience."[60]

Paul Dewar's dyslexia was acknowledged and he received help with it, but Bob Dewar's was not. (Bob was born in 1952, and literature on and treatment for dyslexia burgeoned in the 1970s rather than in the 1960s when Bob would have needed help.[61]) Cathy Dewar believes that she also suffered from dyslexia, but that it was ignored because she was a girl.

Cathy Dewar is likely correct and, moreover, it could be that Marion Dewar herself was affected by the problem. Marion had been an outstanding student, but she always had difficulty with French,[62] which may have been a sign of a learning disability because dyslexics often encounter severe problems when they attempt to learn a second language.[63] (When she was young, Marion's father always encouraged her to learn French, but that did not happen. When she tried out her French on francophone girls she knew, they would switch to English. As an adult, she was critical of the shabby treatment the francophone majority received in the Buckingham of her youth, but she still struggled with the language herself.) Bob Dewar thinks his grandfather, Wilson Bell, suffered from a learning disability. When Bob saw Wilson's address book after his death in 1978, "everything was spelled out phonetically." Bob is convinced this was not because of his grandfather's limited formal education.

The Dewar household was never calm or trouble-free. From the beginning, there was Ken's problem with alcohol. He struggled with it all his life, and so did Marion. She never wanted to be a woman like June Cleaver, the archetypical suburban housewife in the popular American television show *Leave It to Beaver*. As historian Joan Sangster said about her, "June Cleaver – the middle-class suburban homemaker...had become a symbol of the wife and mother who worked in the home...." The June Cleaver character "celebrated the security of traditional gender roles for men and women."[64] Marion Dewar was generous, honest, open, and committed to an unusually high standard of right-thinking behaviour. But she was also quick-tempered and even exacting at times. And none of the four children – although they have all become unusually engaging, interesting, and successful adults – were youngsters without problems or conflicts with their parents. Nonetheless, this family functioned well, largely because at its centre was a remarkably successful marriage. Ken wrote the following to Marion on her birthday in 1988:

> Happy Birthday from your husband, companion, sparring partner, confidant, bridge partner, and, I hope, your best friend.
> All My Love, Ken
> Modesty prevents me from mentioning my other titles.[65]

While there were stresses and strains between the two of them, their love and commitment to each other overrode the problems that confronted them. In fact, their love deepened during a marriage that not only endured but remained vibrant during more than half a century. As their friend Robert Fox told me, "They were in love their whole lives." Or, as their daughter Cathy put it in an anniversary card she wrote them sometime in the 1970s, "Your marriage gives us hope and encouragement about what can happen when two people unconditionally commit to working, sharing and enjoying each other's friendship and love."[66]

The Dewar household was not only characterized by lively open discussions; their house was also open to many needy people, most of them young. Bob Dewar told me that when he was a young man, coming home to Rex Avenue could lead to unexpected surprises. "You never knew who you would trip over." In fact, there was a revolving door of people coming into and out of the house. Marion and Ken might be housing an American draft resister fleeing the Vietnam War or providing a refuge for a neighbourhood young person such as Giselle Bertrand, who was from a struggling family that lived just behind them on Rex Avenue.

The Dewars continued to open up their home in this way even after their own children were grown. In 1985 they provided a home for Elaine Morris, who came to live with them when she was sixteen. Elaine Morris was from Jamaica. Both her parents had died when she was fourteen. She knew Cathy Dewar first, and Cathy married her brother, but it was Marion who arranged to sponsor her and bring her to Ottawa. Elaine was like a daughter to her. "Marion was a lovely human being. She was my mother." Ken "was definitely a father.… It was home." The Dewars also took in a number of men who needed refuge because they had left the priesthood. In the 1990s, when Sudan was in a state of virtual civil war, the Dewar home became a safe house for Sudanese men.

FROM TRADITIONAL TO RADICAL CATHOLICISM

Marion Dewar was a private person during the first two decades of her married life, defining herself primarily as a wife and mother. But she was more than that. Marion and Ken were both devout Catholics. And beginning in 1960, four years after they moved to Rex Avenue, they were fortunate enough to have access to St. Basil's Church, an extraordinary Catholic parish. Their connection to St. Basil's would be central to both of them for the rest of their lives and it would have a transformative effect on Marion.

Marion Dewar attended Mass almost daily all her adult life, but her definition of her faith changed radically over the years. The little girl who was awed by the pre-Second Vatican Council pomp and solemnity of St.-Grégoire de Naziance in Buckingham became an outspoken radical who supported the ordination of women, birth control, and a woman's right to choose abortion. St. Basil's had much to do with her ability to redefine her faith over six decades and yet remain a practising Catholic.

St. Basil's, just a few minutes' walk from their house, was very much a post-Second Vatican Council Church and congregation. It was built "in the round" and dedicated to an open, vital, modernized form of Catholicism. Paul Dewar remembers the folk Masses held at the church and a performance of *Jesus Christ Superstar*.

From its founding in 1956 until 1992, St. Basil's was run by the Basilian order. The Basilian order dates from nineteenth-century France. The order is known for its commitment to outreach. The first priest at St. Basil's was the extraordinary Father Anthony John Ruth. Ruth began life as a farm boy in Ontario. Born in 1914, he was one of nine children in a devout Catholic family. Like several of his sisters and brothers, he went into the church. Educated at

Ken and Marion Dewar shake hands with Pope John Paul II. Note Marion's proper go-to-church hat, and sober dress. Although she became increasingly radical as a Catholic, Marion Dewar remained a Catholic.

St. Michael's College, University of Toronto, he went on to ordination in 1942 as a Basilian father.[67] Father Ruth was a hardworking, approachable, and loveable man. Years later Dewar reminisced about the "big effect" Father Ruth had on her and how he got her involved in social action through the church and St. Basil's parish. John Ruth served as priest from 1958 to 1964 and from 1970 to 1979, and then remained from 1980 to 1987 as semi-retired. In his later years in Ottawa, he stayed with the Dewars.

As Marion described it, he visited her one evening at home and told her about the plight of a neighbouring family. Rex Avenue was still rural in 1960, and the father of the family was a farmhand for a man who farmed land just behind the Dewars' house. (Rex Avenue was named for the farmer's dog.) The farmhand's family was so poor that the children could not go to school, because the family could not provide clothing for them. "That's awful, Father," Marion said to Father Ruth. Father Ruth's response was that he could not do anything about this situation, but that he knew she could. "He knew

I was a nurse," Marion remembered. "So then we organized and we had the women going in and so forth."[68]

Bob Dewar recalls that it was mainly his mother who went into the house to help. The farmhand's wife did not have basic housekeeping skills. Marion showed her how to scrub a floor and how to wash diapers. Kind, compassionate, down-to-earth Marion, we can surmise, knew how to help – with advice as well as with practical tasks – without being intrusive or patronizing. This was the first but not the last time that Father Ruth called on her for assistance with a family in trouble. Dewar, with the support of Father Ruth, widened her efforts. It was she more than any other parishioner at St. Basil's who was responsible for the formation of St. Basil's Social Action Committee, and she, with Ken's support, devoted an enormous amount of effort to it.[69]

Bob Dewar recollects that the motto of St. Basil's Social Action Committee was "What would Jesus do?" The answer was that Jesus would act. And that is what the St. Basil's Social Action Committee did, helping needy neighbours in the community with food and with practical matters, like housekeeping or companionship. As Marion recalled years later, "We didn't help…a lot of families, but we helped them in depth."[70] And as Joan White, a neighbour of the Dewars, told me, the Dewars were "parents to everybody" and "open to everybody," including people who came to the Rex Avenue neighbourhood "from other countries." Dewar did not restrict herself to the neighbourhood or to St. Basil's Social Action Committee. She "used to go downtown and help out as a volunteer in a street clinic for young drug addicts." Taking action suited Marion Dewar's inclinations and temperament. It was always the case for Dewar that if she saw a problem, she would attempt to fix it right then and there.

Another St. Basil's parish group, the Christian Family Movement (CFM), had an even greater effect than the Social Action Committee in shaping Marion's transition from Catholic housewife to public figure. The Christian Family Movement was a group designed to encourage the exploration of new patterns of observance among Catholic married couples. In the United States and Canada it blossomed after the Second Vatican Council, although it was established before that. The St. Basil's CFM was initiated in 1959, just before the Second Vatican Council. It was the first one to be established in Ottawa.[71]

Marion Dewar with her campaign team. She was running for mayor for the first time. C. October 1978. Note the ashtray, as well as the coffee cups. Marion was a smoker, but she quit smoking in the early 1980s.

The credo of the Christian Family Movement was "Observe, Judge, Act." At the heart of CFM were informal groups of couples. They met in turn at members' houses. The group would study the scriptures and discuss issues, Mass would be celebrated in the house, and everyone would enjoy a potluck supper.[72] A priest would attend, but his role was to remain silent and make comments only at the end of the meeting. Father Corbin Eddy remembers that the priest who attended the CFM group in which the Dewars were involved was often Father Gordon Irving, a sociology professor, first at St. Patrick's College in Ottawa and then at Carleton University.

The group to which the Dewars belonged served as a place for Catholic couples to discuss questions that might be troubling them. These included the position of women in the church. We can surmise that the CFM encouraged Marion Dewar's faith to become deeper and more vivid. It also most likely inspired her to become more radical, both as a woman and as a Catholic. For Dewar, the CFM did indeed centre on the family – not on the inward-looking family, but rather on the role the family needed to play in repairing the world.

Father Corbin Eddy, who was the ninth pastor of St. Basil's from 1992 to 2000, knew Marion and Ken Dewar well.[73] Marion, by the time he knew her, was radical in her beliefs about women and the church, most obviously as a supporter of the ordination of women, of birth control, and of a woman's right to choose to have an abortion. But her relationship to her children was also radical, Father Eddy said. Marion Dewar believed that we cannot know what our children will do, and they do not belong to us in any case. Ken took the same position. "As to their kids," Father Eddy told me, "there was always an atmosphere of dialogue and discussion in the family, and unconditional acceptance of them in their adventures, even misadventures." Today, Bob, Liz, and Cathy practise no religion. Paul attends the United Church of Canada, but he remains a Catholic and attends Mass occasionally at St. Basil's. Father Eddy commented that while Marion and Ken would have liked all their children to remain Catholic, "they would give them unconditional support for whatever decisions they would make...."

In 1983, when Dewar was mayor, she received a letter from a correspondent who asked her why she remained a Catholic, rather than leaving the Church as he had done, to fight "its ridiculous, out-dated policies concerning abortion, birth control, divorce, male supremacy and sexual morality." Dewar answered him at length: "I share many of your specific concerns, and have chosen to fight for them from within the church...I think it unfortunate that you have not chosen to fight the church from within, where it must respond to you as a parishioner, but can assure you that I am working for the same goals...."[74]

She gave a similar answer to her son Paul, when he was in university and he asked her, "How can you be a member of an organization that oppresses women...?" She answered, "It is my church: no one will tell me what it is."

In fact, Dewar's evolution from traditional to radical Catholicism was not easy either for her or for the priests she knew who protected her. Robert Fox says that there was no way the church hierarchy would admonish Marion Dewar, even though some did disagree with her – she was, after all, the "poster child for belief." But others say that by the 1980s, many people – priests and parishioners – objected so strongly to her radicalism that they thought she should be censured and even excommunicated. As one such angry Catholic put it, when discussing a conference held in 2005 that called for the ordination of women and at which Marion Dewar gave the welcoming address, "These women are not solely interested in ordination or finding a bishop to obey; they want a *different* church from that of Jesus Christ.... Unfortunately, many priests and laity do not understand that these women have left the Catholic Church both in spirit and in deed."[75]

Paul Dewar commented that Father John Ruth protected her. "Archbishop Plourde [of Ottawa] went to Father Ruth, asked him to get Mum to stop. 'She needs to understand what our position is on abortion.' Father Ruth never went to Mum. He protected her."

Dewar's views on abortion did indeed evolve from the traditional Catholic position of opposition to support for a woman's right to choose. It is clear that Dewar would never have had an abortion herself. Abortion, Robert Fox told me, was "personally for her a painful issue." But it was the "viciousness of the pro-life movement, its blinkeredness," which made her come out in favour of choice. Marion Dewar's niece Gail told me that while her mother, Olive, was never pro-choice, her Aunt Marion convinced Gail that women do have a right to choose abortion. Opposition to abortion for oneself "doesn't mean it [abortion] must be wrong for everybody."

Dewar's radicalization as a Catholic did not come about through reading feminist theological writings like those of Rosemary Radford Ruether, for example, who in 1974 stated bluntly that the Judeo-Christian tradition promoted "misogynism" and "is undoubtedly the single most important shaper and enforcer of the image and role of women in culture and society."[76] Marion was well aware of the Second Vatican Council, but there is no evidence that she read about that either. She did read some theology, including some of the works of the Jesuit thinker Pierre Teilhard de Chardin. Ken read his works as well, and he and Marion discussed them. She also read Victor Frankl's influential 1962 book *Man's Search for Meaning*, which was first published in German in 1946. And she read Riane Eisler's 1987 work, *The Chalice and the Blade: Our History, Our Future*. Bob Dewar remembers that this book had a profound influence on her. Eisler's book advocates the feminine as life-giving and finds historical precedent in goddess worship in the Paleolithic and Neolithic periods. My guess is that she had read Eisler by the time Hofmann Nemiroff interviewed her in the mid-1990s, because she told Hofmann Nemiroff that when she did envision God in human form, She was always a woman. But Dewar's evolution from traditional to feminist Catholic came about primarily through her experience.

PUBLIC HEALTH NURSING AND AN "ETHIC OF CARE"

St. Basil's Church historian, Catherine Casserly, believes that the Christian Family Movement played a part in Marion Dewar's decision to enter public life: "Together each cell pondered many questions. One was the role of women in the church...Marian [sic] Dewar's reaction was to run for city council."[77]

The Christian Family Movement did contribute to Marion Dewar's evolution from wife, mother, and volunteer activist to public figure. But before her public career began in 1972, she also undertook a significant professional transition.

In the 1950s and 1960s, while she was raising her children and expanding her charitable activities from neighbourliness to organized social action, primarily through St. Basil's Social Action Committee and the CFM, she did continue to work, nursing one shift a week. This was an unusual choice during a period when the prevailing ideology decreed that middle-class mothers were not supposed to be in the workforce. However, by the mid-1960s, when Paul, her youngest child, was about to start school, she decided she needed more paid work and more training. The field she chose, public health nursing, was a perfect fit for her skills, talents, and character strengths.

Public health has a long history. During the European Black Death in the fourteenth century, village and town authorities saw to the removal of dead bodies in the hope of restricting the spread of infection. The use of Edward Jenner's smallpox vaccination in the eighteenth century represents a pioneering effort in immunization. By the late nineteenth century, public health advocates lobbied for clean water, clean air, and the removal of "noxious" houses, which meant, in effect, slum clearance.

Nurses played a part in public health only when nursing became a profession in the late nineteenth and early twentieth centuries.

Before that, nursing in Protestant Europe and North America had been an occupation for women with no training, who were commonly thought to be not "respectable." In Catholic areas there were, of course, nuns who were nursing sisters, but they did not practise as public health nurses, although they sometimes visited the sick poor in their own homes.

By the mid-twentieth century, when Marion trained as a nurse in the 1940s and in public health in the 1960s, public health nursing in North America was flourishing. Public health, like medicine in general, was strongly influenced during these years by the belief that medicine had become genuinely "scientific." Doctors and nurses believed that antibiotics were lifesavers: the harm that the overprescribing of antibiotics could do – a common theme in the twenty-first century – was not part of mid-twentieth-century medical discourse. Doctors, nurses, and laypeople accepted and were grateful for the benefits of immunization. The Salk vaccine against polio, for example, first introduced in the 1950s, was a major landmark.

Public health interventions in North America were also strongly influenced by a belief that the family was a cornerstone of North American life. As one public health writer put it, "Well-adjusted, happy families improve the moral fibre of our nation. We are, in a sense, founded on the premise that the family is the most important unit of our culture. Good nursing service implies the application of modern, scientific nursing counselling to meet the health needs of families."[78]

Public health nursing in the mid-twentieth century usually involved going into someone's home. If you heard the doorbell ring and refused to let the nurse come in, you'd have a problem, even if you experienced her visit as an invasion of your privacy. Marion Dewar, I suggest, would have been a public health visitor who recognized the dangers of trespassing and the necessity of collaboration between nurse, patient, and family. She had, after all, been respectful and sensitive when she was a volunteer, both through St. Basil's Church and within the community.

What did public health nurses actually do? As the remarkable Dr. Marie Loyer, who taught Child and Maternal Health in the University of Ottawa's Public Health Certificate training program, said wryly, when I had the privilege of interviewing her, "Nobody records what people do as public health nurses...because it's 'insignificant.' But it's the foundation of being healthy." Loyer went on to become dean of nursing at the University of Ottawa, but in the 1960s she was involved in the Public Health Certificate program. Loyer is another radical Catholic. I asked her, "When will the church accept birth control?" Her answer; "When there are women priests."

In the mid-twentieth century, the province of Ontario, which wanted more public health nurses, paid for a program in which a registered nurse could earn a certificate in public health nursing. From the 1940s until 1971, the University of Ottawa offered such a one-year certificate, and Marion took this course in 1967–1968.[79] The registered nurses in this program were all mature students, Marie Loyer recollects, and they were nearly all women. They worked hard and Loyer and others made sure that they got a thorough understanding of public health as well as clinical training.

Loyer remembers Marion Dewar well. What she remembers most clearly was her outspoken, passionate support for birth control. Loyer was sympathetic. As a young woman, she herself had worked as a public health nurse in the Prescott-Russell and Stormont-Dundas regions of Ontario. Loyer remembers that "often the barn was in much better shape than the house, and the woman/mother would have little in the way of resources or care."

Later, when she studied at Columbia University in New York City, Loyer worked in public health in Harlem and Spanish Harlem. She often dealt with families in which the mother had too many children and not enough knowledge. In the late 1960s, advocating birth control was radical and even risky if you were a Catholic. Dewar was in the same certificate program class as another Catholic woman who was opposed to birth control. This woman created severe problems for Marie Loyer.

After earning her public health certificate in 1968, Marion began working as a public health nurse for the Victorian Order of Nurses (VON). That extraordinary organization was founded in 1897. For more than a century it has provided Canadians with community nursing and public health services. [80]

Did public health nursing in the 1960s and 1970s speak with a feminist voice? Support for women's access to birth control from women like Dewar, Loyer, and Helen Chesterman (author of "The

Public Health Nurse and Family Planning"), should indeed be seen as advocacy for women, but it should not be construed as feminist. In the mid-twentieth century, nursing as a profession did not challenge the male-dominated family, nor did it question the belief that nurses were to be "subordinate helpmeets" to physicians. "The hands of a nurse are the physician's hands lengthened out to minister to the sick," as one nurse put it in 1893. In the mid-twentieth century, this hierarchical notion still prevailed.[81]

Recently, feminist historians have seen a proto-feminist side to the Victorian Order of Nurses, dating back to the Order's founding in the 1890s; this arose from fierce opposition to, rather than support for, the VON. Many late-Victorian Canadian physicians did not support the VON at first because they were afraid that the nurses would have too much autonomy. As the Ontario Medical Association put it in June 1897, "After careful consideration of the scheme for the founding of the Victorian Order of Nurses...the Ontario Medical Association...feels that it would be neglecting a serious duty if it failed to express its most unqualified disapproval of the scheme, on account of the dangers which must necessarily follow...."[82]

It was only in the late twentieth century that nursing in North America adopted a clearly articulated feminist position, one that nursing historian Susan Malka rightly says involves a feminist "ethic of care." Nurses as a group have become assertive about their conditions of work and more outspoken about proclaiming that nursing is not the same as medical doctoring: It is an autonomous profession focused on caring as much as on curing.

Marion's own evolution from a supporter of women to a feminist came earlier, developing gradually in the 1970s and flourishing by the 1980s, as we shall see in the following chapters.

ENDNOTES:

[49] *The Buckingham Post*, two-column story; *Papineau County Echo*, September 21, 1951 (paid announcement). My thanks to Linda Cameron for sending me this. She got it with the help of Nancy Renaud.

[50] Ernest Kurtz, *Not-God: A History of Alcoholics Anonymous* (Center City, MN: Hazelden Educational Services, 1979); Klaus Makela et al, *Alcoholics Anonymous as a Mutual-Help Movement: A Study in Eight Societies* (Madison, WI: University of Wisconsin Press, 1996); Norman K. Denzin, *The Alcoholic Self* (Newbury Park, CA: Sage Publications, 1987). There is extensive literature on alcohol and alcoholism and on the emergence of Alcoholics Anonymous, the first and most powerful "12-step" group in North America.

[51] Bette S. Tallen, "Codependency: A Feminist Critique," in *Challenging Codependency: Feminist Critiques*, eds. Marguerite Babcock and Christine McKay (Toronto: University of Toronto Press, 1995), 171.

[52] Denzin, passim.

[53] Grazyna Zajdow, *Al-Anon Narratives, Women, Self-Stories, and Mutual Aid.* (Westport, CT: Greenwood Press, 2002), 4.

[54] See Babcock and McKay, eds.

[55] See Zaidow, 14.

[56] Hofmann Nemiroff interview.

[57] Ibid.

[58] City of Ottawa Archives, Marion Dewar Fonds, A 2010-0765, folder 1. Letter from "Miss Cathy Dewar, c/o Camp Tekakwitha," summer 1970.

[59] Hofmann Nemiroff interview. Marion Dewar talks frankly about this and about her charitable work in drug addiction.

[60] City of Ottawa Archives, Marion Dewar Fonds, A2010-0766, folder 16, June 4, 1978 letter from "Celia," who also had a boy at Gow. She had seen Marion and Ken at "Gow Parents Day." Celia praises Gow and its success: "some boys can go to college/university" she says. I found this letter both touching and amusing: I first knew Paul Dewar when he was a university student at Carleton University, and I was a professor of history. He took a course from me, which was a pleasure for me and I think for him. When I read that letter, I thought: yes, and some Gow students go on to become Members of Parliament.

[61] Linda S. Siegel, "Perspectives on Dyslexia," *Journal of Paediatrics and Child Health*. Nov 2006; 11(9): 581–587, on the history of dyslexia and its treatment.

[62] *Lux Glebiana*, 1945, the Glebe Collegiate Institute Yearbook. Florence Berndt kindly let me see Marion Dewar's entry, which includes: "Pet Aversion: French." When she was mayor she did her best to improve her French,

spending time at the Centre Linguistique at Jonquière, in the Saguenay region of Quebec. See also City of Ottawa Archives, Marion Dewar Fonds, A2010-0765, folder 6, "Mayor's Personal Correspondence" 198, for example, her letter of 12/5/1983. However, her knowledge of French remained limited.

[63] Ganshow, Leonore, Sparks, Richard L. and Javorsky, James (1998) "Foreign Language Learning Difficulties: An Historical Perspective." *Journal of Learning Disabilities*, 31: 248-258.

[64] Joan Sangster, "Doing Two Jobs: The Wage-Earning Mother, 1945–1970" in *A Diversity of Women: Ontario, 1945–1980*, ed. Joy Parr, (Toronto: University of Toronto Press, 1995), 98–134, 102.

[65] City of Ottawa Archives, Marion Dewar Fonds, A 2010-0765, folder 1, see the "Thunderbird" card.

[66] City of Ottawa Archives, Marion Dewar Fonds, A 2010-0765, folder 1, Cathy's letter.

[67] Catherine M. Casserly, *St. Basil's Parish, 1956-2006: Our Jubilee Journey*, manuscript, 2008. Casserly kindly let me keep a photocopy of the manuscript. See Chapter 4 on Father Ruth, 23–28 of manuscript.

[68] Hofmann Nemiroff interview.

[69] Casserly, *St. Basil's Parish,* 61; St. Basil's Social Action Committee dates from the early 1960s. Janine Brodie, *Women and Politics in Canada* (Toronto: McGraw Hill-Ryerson Ltd, 1985), 51 and following. Brodie points out the importance of volunteer work for women who then went on to politics, most often municipal politics.

[70] Hofmann Nemiroff interview.

[71] Casserly, 36: "St. Basil's was the first parish in Ottawa to establish CFM and it led the way for other parishes. The seed was sown by Father Ruth and quickly grew." For the CFM in the US and Canada, see Jeffrey M. Burns, *Disturbing the Peace: A History of the Christian Family Movement, 1949-1974* (Notre Dame, IN: University of Notre Dame Press, 1999).

[72] Susan B. Whitney, *Mobilizing Youth: Communists and Catholics in Interwar France* (Durham, NC: Duke University Press, 2009), 90–92 and passim. The CFM owed much to the Observe, Judge, Act formula for Catholic Action developed by Belgian Canon Joseph Cardijn.

[73] Father Eddy performed the funeral Mass and delivered the eulogy for Ken in 2003 and for Marion in 2008.

[74] City of Ottawa Archives, Marion Dewar Fonds, A2010-0765, folder 6, Letter from J. Douglas Bourne to Dewar, 10/ 29/1983; and her reply 11/21/1983.

[75] http://catholicculture.org/culture/library/view.cfm?recnum=6650, comment from Donna O'Connor-Hunnisett, ocds, "Women's Ordination World Wide Conferences I and II" accessed June 4, 2016.

[76] Rosemary Radford Ruether, ed., *Religion & Sexism: Images of Women in the Jewish and Christian Traditions* (New York: Simon and Schuster, 1974), 9.

[77] Casserly, 37. "Cell" was the term CFM used for the family groups.

[78] Helen Chesterman, "The Public Health Nurse and Family Planning," in *Public Health Nursing: A Book of Readings*, Dorothy M. Stewart and Pauline A. Vincent, eds., (Dubuque, IA: Wm. C. Brown Company Publishers, 1968), 166. Chesterman goes on to advocate the teaching of birth control. This book of readings was in the University of Ottawa nursing library at the time Dewar studied there. On public health nursing in Canada see Beverly Boutilier, "Helpers or Heroines? The National Council of Women, Nursing, and 'Woman's Work' in Late Victorian Canada" and Meryn Stuart, "Shifting Professional Boundaries: Gender Conflict in Public Health, 1920-1925" in *Caring and Curing: Historical Perspectives on Women and Healing in Canada*, Dianne Dodd and Deborah Gorham, eds. (Ottawa: University of Ottawa Press, 1994).

[79] École des Sciences Infirmières de L'université D'Ottawa *1933-1973 The University of Ottawa School of Nursing* (Ottawa: University of Ottawa Press, 1973). See 72 for Dewar's completion of the Public Health Certificate in 1968.

[80] Hofmann Nemiroff interview. Dewar says she worked for the VON after she got her Public Health Certificate. For the founding of the VON see Beverly Boutilier, "Gender, Organized Women, and the Politics of Institution Building: Founding of the Victorian Order of Nurses for Canada, 1893–1900," Ph.D., Carleton University, Ottawa, 1993. The VON told me that they do not have employment records for the 1960s so there appears to be no way to verify Dewar's employment with them.

[81] Boutilier (1994), 20; and Stuart quoting Isabel Hampton, 51.

[82] Quoted in John Murray Gibbon, *The Victorian Order of Nurses: 50th Anniversary: 1987-1947* (Montreal: The Victorian Order of Nurses for Canada, 1947), 12. Among the recent feminist historians: Boutilier and Stuart.

Marion Dewar, in cap and gown, proudly holds her diploma. She's receiving her bachelor's degree in public health from the University of Ottawa in 1972. Her son Bob stands to the right of his mother, family friends Kay and Peter Marshall are on her left.

Chapter 3
ENTERING PUBLIC LIFE

In 1972, Marion Dewar earned her degree in public health from the University of Ottawa. She had been working as a public health nurse since completing her one-year certificate in 1968, but getting the degree took four more years of part-time study. The province of Ontario had funded the certificate, but she had to pay for the University of Ottawa degree courses. Earning this degree was a significant achievement. Not only did it increase her status as a public health nurse, it increased her knowledge and her self-confidence.

A POLITICAL MENTOR: PAULINE JEWETT

In 1972, Dewar also became involved in politics, at first as a volunteer, a role with which she was, of course, familiar. In the summer and fall of 1972, Dewar worked for New Democratic Party (NDP) candidate Pauline Jewett. Jewett conducted a spirited campaign for the federal seat in Ottawa West, and Dewar ran fundraising coffee parties and had her first experience canvassing door to door.

Pauline Jewett's career and personal life provide a striking contrast to Dewar's. Born in 1922, she was just a few years older than Dewar. The Jewett family's social, cultural, and economic status was higher than that of the Bells. Jewett's parents – and in particular her father, in sharp contrast to the authoritarian and irascible Wilson Bell, who told his daughter she could not go to Queen's – encouraged her to pursue an academic career. Jewett successfully completed high school at St. Catharines Collegiate (in St. Catharines, Ontario) doing "well enough to win an entrance scholarship to Queen's University." She entered Queen's in the fall of 1940 and graduated in the spring of 1944, with "first-class honours in political science and philosophy."[83]

Jewett did outstandingly well as an undergraduate, but Queen's was not an easy place for women in the mid-twentieth-century decades. "An entrenched, accepted prejudice that women were somehow second-class students persisted." Female faculty had an even more difficult time than female students.[84] Pauline Jewett was fortunate, however, because she received encouragement and support from some key figures at Queen's, among them the remarkable Jean Royce, the university registrar.[85]

Pauline Jewett went on to pursue a Ph.D. at Harvard University, beginning her studies in 1945 and receiving her degree in 1949. She landed a permanent academic position not at Queen's, as she had hoped she might, but at the new Carleton College in Ottawa in 1955. (It became Carleton University in 1957.)

Jewett's biographer comments that "Pauline held the inveterate belief that the Parliament of Canada was important and did indeed matter."[86] By 1959 she had decided to go into politics, aiming to run for a seat in Canada's federal parliament. Although she did consider affiliating with the New Democratic Party (which she would join later), it was the Liberals she joined in 1959. As journalist and broadcaster Peter Gzowski put it in 1962, "Like many other academics, she was urged – and somewhat inclined – to join the New [Democratic] Party, in its embryonic stages. But after more than a year of mind-searching…she decided her sympathies were with the Liberals."[87]

Jewett ran and was elected MP for the Ontario riding of Northumberland in 1963, and she sat as a Liberal until her defeat in the election of 1965. Her defeat meant a return to academic life, but she re-entered politics in the 1970s, switching parties. She ran for the New Democrats unsuccessfully in Ottawa West in 1972. In 1979 she would win a federal seat in British Columbia and serve in Parliament until 1988.

Why did Jewett switch parties? One reason may be that she objected to Prime Minister Trudeau's imposition of the War Measures Act during the October Crisis of 1970. But there were, one can surmise, other reasons. Jewett was ambitious: she did not want to be a backbencher. She wanted a cabinet post, and the Liberals were not going to give it to her.

Working for Jewett's campaign brought about a sea change in Dewar. As she would later say, "In many ways she [Jewett] was my role model and mentor. Her thinking about what women should do and could do was very much an inspiration. I remember thinking, 'Now here is Dr. Jewett talking to little old me, mostly suburban housewife, asking me what I think.' It was extremely empowering."[88]

Political scientist and New Democratic Party activist Jill Vickers points out that if Dewar was "empowered" by Pauline Jewett, in return Jewett learned a lot from Dewar. "Jewett," says Vickers, "never really understood feminist politics.... Pauline wasn't very comfortable with ordinary people." In contrast, Dewar was "direct, warm. One time, after an encounter at the door, Pauline said to Marion, 'We're not supposed to talk about local politics.' Marion replied 'But that's what she wanted to talk about.'" Vickers believes, though, that Jewett taught Marion Dewar a lot about federal politics, about the legislative context, and about foreign policy.

Working on Jewett's campaign not only introduced Dewar to politics, it turned her into a staunch, lifelong New Democrat. The federal NDP, which came in third in the October 1972 elections, was then led by the redoubtable David Lewis. Dewar was introduced to the party's platform, with its support for social justice, when she campaigned for Jewett in 1972. The 1972 NDP platform included: promises to end "corporate welfare" and use the money for housing, transportation, and municipal services; a pledge to control profits and rents, but not wages; a public works fund for the winter months, to reduce unemployment; a reduction in income tax rates for low-income and middle-class Canadians; and an increase in old age security payments. The principles of the NDP struck an immediate and lasting chord with Dewar.

DEWAR'S ENTRY INTO LOCAL POLITICS
In sharp contrast to Jewett, who started at the top, it was to local, rather than federal or provincial, politics that Dewar would turn when she became active herself. This was not an unusual choice for someone with Dewar's background. As political scientist Janine

Brodie points out, "Volunteer groups played an important role in the political socialization and education of women candidates, especially those who eventually sought a career in municipal politics."[89] Late in 1972, at the urging of Dr. Ralph Sutherland, an NDP stalwart who had served as alderman for Carleton Ward from 1970 to 1972,[90] Dewar agreed to run for alderman herself. It appears from comments in the press at the time, and from Dewar's own later recollections, that it was her experience as a public health nurse in Britannia that pushed her in the direction of politics. She had been appalled by what she saw when she visited families there. More health and social initiatives were desperately needed in the schools and in the community. As she recalled years later, she had told her husband, "For two cents, I'd run for council."[91]

Dewar ran her first campaign for alderman of the newly created Britannia Ward "on a shoestring."[92] She raised small amounts among many friends and supporters throughout Ottawa and farther afield. They included such NDP notables as Evelyn Gigantes and Montrealer F.R. Scott.[93] Although she was not planning on winning (this was her first time as a candidate, after all), she did. In the municipal elections held on December 4, 1972, Dewar ran against nine other candidates and came first.

The civic elections received extensive coverage in the press. Of Dewar, the *Ottawa Citizen* said:

> Although she lives two blocks out of her ward, public health nurse Mrs. Marion Dewar says she has become familiar with its problems through her professional and volunteer work in Britannia.... She says the ward needs a lot of new recreational facilities and predicts that provincially-sponsored community health centres will soon become a reality.[94]

When Marion Dewar entered local politics, Ottawa was not today's sprawling Ottawa-Carleton, with its rural and urban areas and its population of over 900,000. But the city already had a multilevel structure. There was the federal presence, manifest most notably through the National Capital Commission. The Regional Municipality of Ottawa-Carleton had been established in 1969.[95] It was to administer services that crossed local boundaries. All the Ottawa aldermen – sixteen including the mayor in 1972 – sat, *ex officio*, on the Council of the Regional Municipality of Ottawa-Carleton. Ottawa also had a Board of Control, made up of four individuals plus the mayor. The board members were elected city-wide. The thought was that controllers would bring a broader scrutiny to pertinent issues than would representatives of a single ward.

A reader of John Taylor's fine history of Ottawa learns that change has always been the story of the city.[96] In the 1830s, when the Rideau Canal was constructed, it was called Bytown. It became Ottawa when it gained incorporation in 1855. It was a rough lumber town then and remained so even after Queen Victoria chose it as Canada's capital in 1857. During the Second World War the federal civil service grew, and in the post-war years so did the suburbs. Tension between federal and municipal jurisdictions arose, reflecting the fact that Ottawa was, as it remains today, both the capital of Canada and a city in its own right.

What impact did growth and the restructuring of local government have on local politics? Douglas Fullerton, former chairman of the National Capital Commission, commented as follows in 1974: "Local power has almost disappeared now…'Mayor of Ottawa' is nothing but a fancy title and a chain of office." He was overstating his case, but he did have a point. Fullerton made this comment in an interview he gave to the *Citizen* on the occasion of the appearance of the Fullerton Report, his study of the governance of the national capital region.[97]

In 1974 the *Citizen* ran an editorial on the office of alderman: "The good alderman – be he male or female – must be a ward man: he must be able to solve problems for his constituents. But he must also represent the city on regional council. So he must have a vision which stretches beyond ward boundaries. He must also be able to give the job a great deal of his time…."[98]

DEWAR'S CONCERN WITH HEALTH, PUBLIC HOUSING, AND ORGANIZED LABOUR

Running in 1972, when aldermen received $9,000 a year, Dewar promised to work "full-time."[99] She fulfilled this promise. As alderman for Britannia Ward, she was hardworking, effective, and attentive to her constituents. She fought for public health issues, securing, for example, free dental care for children who needed it, even if their parents were not on welfare, and she established herself as an opponent of growth for growth's sake and as a supporter of public transportation.[100]

The first woman to sit on a Canadian municipal council was Annie Gale, elected in Calgary in 1917.[101] In 1972, when Dewar was elected, she was the only woman on Ottawa's council. Across Canada, women made up less than seven per cent of those involved in municipal politics. This number would grow over the next two decades, but in 2015 it is still only around 25 per cent.[102] It was a while before Dewar could get up her courage to speak out in this intimidating environment. Bob Dewar told me it was her husband Ken – her most abiding and loyal supporter – who gave her the confidence she needed. Early on in her term as alderman, Ken went to city hall to sit in on a council meeting. Marion was silent. Afterward, he reminded her that she had a lot to say, and he urged her to speak up. With his encouragement, she did.

When I asked former NDP MP Michael Cassidy to comment on Dewar's election and subsequent success as a local politician, he said she earned it and she deserved it: "She was a good and diligent alderman and that was the base from which she rose to run for mayor and win."

In the civic election of 1974, she ran for one of the four Board of Control positions and was not only elected but topped the poll, also becoming, as a result, the deputy mayor. In that election, Lorry Greenberg became mayor, the first Jewish person ever elected to the city's highest office. Greenberg, a member of the Minto construction family, was colourful and outspoken as a man and as the city's mayor. He and Marion Dewar developed a frank and open relationship. They got along well, largely because Dewar was determined that they should.

What did a controller do? In 1974, the *Ottawa Citizen* explained:

Controllers have two board meetings a week, two city council, and two regional council meetings a month. Most are members of at least one hospital board, council committee, or other municipal agency. Traditionally, the controller who receives the most votes is appointed deputy mayor, sits on regional government's

executive committee, and 'fills in' when the
mayor is away.... The deputy mayor gets
$27,600 a year, the other three $21,600.[103]

Evelyn Gigantes and Michael
Cassidy appear on the left of
the picture, along with Marion
Dewar and an unidentified man.

Although Marion Dewar ran as controller
and served from 1974 to 1978, she did support the abolition of the
board when abolition became a hot political issue in 1977. Ironically,
however, her work as controller exemplified the board's positive
features. From the beginning of her tenure as controller, citizen
activists knew that she was the board member with an interest in
women's issues and social issues and that she was skeptical about
growth for growth's sake. She also received letters and telephone
calls concerning immediate and practical matters, such as snow
clearance and zoning.

For some constituents, such mundane concerns were mingled
with broader questions. One constituent who was having problems
with roadwork on Walkley Road (on the outskirts of Ottawa) appreciated her help with that matter, but also praised her for her advocacy
of nurses and patients during the then current health care crisis. "It

is gratifying to know that the people of Ottawa elected a controller having your concern of citizens at heart." He adds that he and his wife, a nurse, were much encouraged by "your show of interest in the Ontario hospital/nursing crisis…. You have our votes."[104]

As alderman, controller, and later mayor, Dewar understood that change could be achieved in many needed areas only at the provincial or federal levels of government, rather than at the municipal level. But she also firmly believed that while municipal and regional politicians could not implement such change, they did have the power of moral suasion.

In 1976, on the health care question, as an unwavering New Democrat she wrote to Stephen Lewis, then leader of the opposition in the Ontario legislature (Progressive Conservative Bill Davis was premier), to urge the NDP to improve its policy on health care. "This is an area that concerns me more than any other," she wrote. "It disturbs me greatly that the NDP does not display stronger feelings about good patient care than any of the other parties. If we had, we would be examining the use of various nursing personnel to do some of the primary care and a strong thrust on prevention. As it is right now," Dewar wrote, "there is gross mismanagement of the health care dollar."[105] Dewar, who was an excellent nurse herself, always believed that the skills of nurses, most of whom were women, were undervalued by the health care system and by the public. As a politician she also came to believe that nurses must play a larger role in the public arena – they must seek to change the world. As she said in a speech on community nursing in March 1985:

> We are often characterized, and come to internalize the description [that we are] helpers to doctors. While we often play a supporting role to the physician, we are also health professionals…. While our responsibility…to our patient is paramount…I believe that our moral obligations go much further. We, of all people…are aware of the importance of the standard of living, the level of individual dignity, to the health of the citizens within our community.[106]

Another cause Dewar supported as controller and later as mayor was the Ottawa Tenants Council for Public Housing, led by the extraordinary activist Dorothy O'Connell. O'Connell, along with her friend and fellow activist Aline Akeson, put pressure on Ottawa's city council to do more for public housing tenants, and especially for their children. When I interviewed Dorothy O'Connell in August of 2013, she had strong praise for Dewar. "I did love the mayor," she told me. "Most people were scared of public housing people then. She was not. She was vitally interested and she didn't make value judgments."[107]

Dewar as controller supported O'Connell and Akeson's Carlingwood Ski Hill program, designed to provide skiing opportunities for children from low-income families living in public housing.[108] Like O'Connell and Akeson, Dewar saw the plight of public housing tenants as a women's issue. After all, it was public-housing mothers who were faced with raising children in constricted surroundings, on limited incomes. O'Connell herself was a strong feminist who defined the problems of public housing in terms of the plight of poor women, often attached to men who did not or could not fulfill their responsibilities as fathers or husbands.

Other groups with feminist interests sought out Dewar's help while she was a controller, including the women behind Interval House[109] – "a not-for-profit safe haven for women and their children fleeing violence," which opened its doors on July 5, 1976. Several community service organizations in Ottawa offered their support, including the Elizabeth Fry Society and Family Services of Ottawa. The committee also asked for and received support from Controller Dewar.

As a firm and principled supporter of organized labour, Dewar also spoke out as controller in defense of Newspaper Guild members involved in a dispute with the *Ottawa Journal,* one of Ottawa's two major newspapers. (This dispute would lead to the paper's demise in 1980.) The conflict began in October 1976, when the *Journal*'s management tried to impose a contract stipulating that the paper's pressmen (the linotype setters) would be supplied by management and not by the International Typographical Union. The unions, led by the Newspaper Guild, resisted. In October 1976, the *Journal*'s management locked out 46 guild members: "In fact they locked out all their unionized employees, including the press room, the composing room, and circulation, which was represented by the Guild. It was a long and nasty strike during which the company ran the paper with non-union personnel."[110] In April 1977, Ottawa's council members voted 8–6 to "to withhold municipal advertising from the *Journal* until the newspaper settles its six-month-old labour dispute." Controller Dewar supported the boycott, even though Mayor Greenberg did not. "I have my conscience to live with," she told the press. "I am looking at the right of people to work."[111] This action earned her no friends among anti-labour colleagues in city government or from anti-labour constituents.[112]

"A WOMEN'S CHOICE" OR "RIGHT TO LIFE"?

In the late 1970s, when she was controller and deputy mayor, Marion Dewar had not fully resolved the painful and difficult conflict between the Catholic beliefs about abortion that she had held as a young woman and the position she would arrive at after a long struggle: support for a woman's right to choose abortion. During her terms as controller, this conflict led her into awkward situations on at least two occasions.

The first occurred in March 1976. She and her friend and fellow local politician Alderman Toddy Kehoe had voted to award a grant of $10,000 to the Ottawa Women's Centre. However, conditions had been attached to this grant: the women's centre would be permitted to display birth control information, but it must also include information from the anti-abortion group Birthright.

Women's centres were established by "women in all parts of the country" in the 1970s. "Feminists viewed such centres…as places where women would connect with the women's movement…. [They] sought birth control and health information, legal advice, feminist therapy, and referrals to doctors who would perform abortions."[113]

But when Alderman Kehoe visited the Ottawa Women's Centre, she did not like what she saw. The centre itself made her uncomfortable. She did not like their prominently displayed poster with its slogan, "A woman needs a man like a fish needs a bicycle." She thought it was anti-male. Moreover, the centre was certainly not displaying any information from Birthright. After her visit, she decided that in good conscience she could no longer support the $10,000 grant, which she then spoke out against in council. She remembered the occasion vividly when I interviewed her in 2013.

Speaking out against the grant had not been easy for her, but she did it, and Marion Dewar backed her up.

John Baglow, then director of the Canadian Alliance to Repeal the Abortion Law, wrote to Dewar to protest her vote at council. In her reply to him she said:

> I understand that the Policy Committee of the Women's Centre advised Alderman Kehoe that there would be both types of literature available.... After she visited the Centre and had strongly supported the grant she discovered there was no literature from Birthright.... It is a genuine concern when any group that obtains grants from the City and makes certain commitments and does not follow through that the status of such a grant is placed in a position of jeopardy.[114]

As Dewar's response indicates, there were freedom of speech questions involved, as Baglow himself, who was usually a Dewar supporter, agreed. But it is possible that in 1976 the underlying reason Dewar and Kehoe objected to the activities of the Ottawa Women's Centre was that they could not, as the Catholics they both were then, tolerate abortion. (When I interviewed her in 2013, Kehoe explained to me that she was no longer a Catholic: "I don't go to church anymore...there are too many men making too many bad decisions.")

The second incident occurred in 1978 when, as deputy mayor (Mayor Greenberg was away), Marion was persuaded to proclaim Friday, May 12, 1978, "Respect for Life" Day. The initiative came from Action Life, an anti-abortion group with strong links to the Catholic Church.

Action Life set up an exhibition at city hall, and spokespeople for the group went into the schools to talk about "Respect for Life." They went to Catholic schools, most notably Immaculata High School, which at that time was a girls' school run by nuns. Many Immaculata girls sent letters like this one to Dewar: "I would like to thank you for having the 'Right for Life Day.' We all are living and we should have a day to appreciate all the good things we have received.... In my opinion no one has the right to take anybody's life away. This is seen when people have an abortion."[115]

But not everyone approved. One correspondent sharply chided

Deputy Mayor Dewar for her proclamation of Respect for Life Day:

> I would like to congratulate you on your stand, if somewhat confused, on abortion. We gather that although you would personally never consider abortion for yourself you would not be against other women having the choice. Like it or not this is clearly a pro-abortion stand as the lines are drawn at the moment. Don't let's camouflage this issue with silly rhetoric – choice is the operative word on this issue.

> Your proclamation marking May 12, 1978, Respect for Life day in Ottawa struck me, therefore, singularly inappropriate...May I suggest that local politicians like yourself stick to the municipal scene rather than dabble in unconnected sensitive areas.[116]

That comment – that local politicians should stick to local issues – ran like a refrain through Dewar's career as alderman, controller, and then mayor.

OTTAWA'S BOARD OF CONTROL IS ABOLISHED

Marion Dewar served as controller from 1974 to 1978. She was then elected mayor in November 1978. One of her first well-publicized acts was to preside over a council meeting abolishing the Board of Control. "A delighted mayor Marion Dewar bangs gavel signaling the end for Ottawa's Board of Control," proclaimed the headline in the *Ottawa Journal*. "The Ottawa Municipal Board has made it official – Ottawa's 76 year old Board of Control will die of old age at the stroke of midnight Nov. 30."[117]

At a distance of almost four decades, the issue of the abolition of Ottawa's Board of Control seems minor, and it is difficult to see what all the fuss was about. There were arguments for retention. The Board of Control members gave Ottawa voters somewhere to go, other than their local alderman or the mayor's office, with complaints, suggestions, and concerns. And Marion Dewar as controller indeed demonstrated the strengths of the office.

In 1977, the arguments for and against retention were laid out in a brief prepared by political scientist Caroline Andrew, acting as a consultant. (Andrew was then at the outset of a distinguished career.) She pointed out that the Board of Control was intended to promote "liberty" but that, in fact, it served as a barrier to effective decision-making. "The decision-making process is at present slow, cumbersome, and multi-level."[118]

Trip Kennedy, one of the aldermen in favour of abolition, wrote about the confusion and delay the board caused: "It is not remarkable that decisions take so long...but rather that any decisions are ever arrived at."[119]

In 1983, Andrew published a piece on Ottawa-Hull, in which she took a retrospective look at the abolition issue. "The abolition of the Board of Control was debated at length," she comments. Andrew asserts that the abolition controversy was important because of what it represented: the effort by "a new generation of activist and largely consumption-oriented politicians to gain control of Ottawa's local government."[120] Those for retention, like Pat Nichol and Don Reid, were, Andrew believes, conservative in outlook and supporters of Ottawa's traditional business interests, especially the interests of real estate developers.

Controller Dewar did not play a major part in this dispute, though she was definitely on the side of abolition. Moreover, she supported consultation. For instance, she tried to convince Mayor Lorry Greenberg that the consultation process about the Board of Control, begun in March 1977, was a valid one. Mayor Greenberg was annoyed by the consultations. He believed that the only voices that would be heard were those of "professional citizens" – people who made a practice of responding in situations like this one. Dewar wrote him a private and informal letter, which speaks volumes about how she cultivated her relationship with Greenberg and tells us as well how strongly she felt about the importance of consultation: "Lorry," she wrote, "we don't want to hear from the 'professional citizens.' Of course not, but we start with people who have some experience with the system but who have been through the war of learning its pitfalls and problems...."[121]

In November 1978, Marion Dewar ran for and was elected mayor.

ENDNOTES:

[83] Judith McKenzie, *Pauline Jewett: A Passion for Canada* (Montreal & Kingston: McGill-Queen's University Press, 1999), 18 and 23.

[84] Ibid, 25.

[85] For Jewett and Royce, see McKenzie, 25–26. For more on Royce and Queen's, see the excellent Robert Hamilton, *Setting the Agenda: Jean Royce and the Shaping of Queen's University* (Toronto: University of Toronto Press, 2002).

[86] McKenzie, xiv.

[87] Peter Gzowski, "The New Women in Politics," *Macleans*, April 21, 1962, quoted in McKenzie, 60.

[88] McKenzie, 155.

[89] Brodie, 53.

[90] Eva Taylor and James Kennedy, *Ottawa's Britannia* (Ottawa: The Britannia Historical Association, 1983), 318.

[91] Hofmann Nemiroff interview.

[92] John Taylor, historian, personal communication.

[93] City of Ottawa Archives, Marion Dewar Fonds, A2010-0769, box # 5, see "Financial Records 1972." By September Dewar had raised $10,783.46.

[94] *Ottawa Citizen*, Friday, December 1, 1972, 66.

[95] Caroline Andrew, "Ottawa-Hull" in *City Politics in Canada*, Warren Magnusson and Andrew Sancton, eds. (Toronto: University of Toronto Press, 1983), 156 and passim. Andrew's article gives an excellent summary of the region's political structure.

[96] John H. Taylor, *Ottawa: An Illustrated History* (Toronto: James Lorimer & Company, 1986).

[97] *Ottawa Citizen*, November 16, 1974, 33. The Fullerton Report, *The Capital of Canada: How Should It Be Governed? A Special Study on the National Capital* (Ottawa: Information Canada, 1974).

[98] *Ottawa Citizen,* November 9, 1974, 6.

[99] See *Ottawa Citizen,* December 1, 1972; 62 for pay and 66 for Dewar.

[100] Taylor and Kennedy, 338.

[101] Annie Gale http://www.heroines.ca/people/gale.html, accessed June 4, 2016.

[102] Lynne A. Weikart, "Politics and the State: North America," in *Routledge*

International Encyclopaedia of Women: Global Women's Issues and Knowledge, Vol 3, Cheris Kramarae and Dale Spender, eds. (London: Routledge, 2000), 1600.

[103] *Ottawa Citizen*, October 29, 1974, 77.

[104] City of Ottawa Archives, Marion Dewar Fonds, A2010-0405 88 2010.0047.1, Letter from A.F. Goetz, 3/25/1976. Goetz was referring to her appearance at a rally for improved health care on March 22, 1976. In 1976, the Pierre Trudeau government was moving toward block funding and Ontario Premier Bill Davis was going along with spending less on health care in Ontario.

[105] City of Ottawa Archives, Marion Dewar Fonds, A 2010-0405 2010.0047.1 88. Letter to Stephen Lewis from Marion Dewar, Controller, City of Ottawa, 10/7/1976.

[106] City of Ottawa Archives, Marion Dewar Fonds, A 2010 0767, box 3, "Speeches, 1985." Speech on Community Nursing given 3/18/1985.

[107] Dorothy O'Connell published her wise and funny novel about women and public housing: *Chicklet Gomez* (Ottawa: Deneau & Greenberg, 1978). The "Greenberg" in Deneau and Greenberg was Irving Greenberg, one of the founders of Minto Construction and brother of Mayor Greenberg.

[108] City of Ottawa Archives, Box 88 A 2010-0405 2010.0047.1, File "Community Groups Ottawa Tenants Council." O'Connell writes to Dewar as Controller on 2/2/1978, and Dewar follows this up with phone calls and support.

[109] See City of Ottawa Archives, Marion Dewar Fonds, Box A2010-0405, folder "Social Services." See correspondence on Interval House.

[110] The Union wants Journal workers decertification bid thrown out," *Ottawa Citizen*, March 9, 1978, 10.

[111] "Greenberg Slams Journal Ad Ban," *Ottawa Citizen,* April 26, 1977, 1. This was after Council voted 8–6 in favour of the ban. See Minutes of the Council of the Corporation of the City of Ottawa, Part 2 (1977), minutes of meeting of 4/18/1977, 1412.

[112] *Ottawa Journal*, October 11, 1978, 63. During the 1978 campaign for the mayoralty, Dewar's opponent Pat Nicol "berated" her for supporting the boycott.

[113] Hamilton (1996), 57.

[114] City of Ottawa Archives, Marion Dewar Fonds, A 2010-0405 2010.0047.1, in box 88. John Baglow to Marion Dewar, March 11, 1976, Dewar's reply, March 28, 1976.

[115] City of Ottawa Archives, Marion Dewar Fonds, A2010-0403, "Respect for Life" folder.

[116] City of Ottawa Archives, Marion Dewar Fonds, A2010-0403, "Respect for

Life" folder, Letter from Lynne Zeitouni 5/16/1978.

[117] City of Ottawa Archives, Marion Dewar Fonds, RG20-8-28 #1. Clipping from the *Ottawa Journal*.

[118] City of Ottawa Archives, Marion Dewar Fonds, RG20-8-28 #1, File 1 contains information on the campaign to abolish the board, including Caroline Andrew's 1977 consultant's report.

[119] City of Ottawa Archives, Marion Dewar Fonds, Box 88 A 2010-0405 2010.0047 1, Brief, 30, Trip Kennedy's brief.

[120] Andrew (1983), 154–155. When Caroline Andrew graciously agreed to meet with me on August 30, 2013, she held to the same position.

[121] City of Ottawa Archives, Marion Dewar Fonds, A 2010-0405 2010.0047, Box 88. Memo in folder 5.

Chapter 4
HER WORSHIP

In the spring of 1978, Lorry Greenberg announced that he would not run again for mayor of Ottawa, and consequently Marion Dewar decided to run herself in the election of November 1978. Her campaign would be a tough one. Dewar's main opponent was Pat Nichol, a fierce and unfriendly adversary. Dewar was by then well known in Ottawa as a local politician of integrity, who advocated for women, poor people, and children. Nichol tried to portray Dewar as a dangerous left-winger, but this tactic did not succeed with voters. The civic election was held on Monday, November 13, 1978. Dewar won handily, outpolling Nichol by more than eighteen thousand votes. Dewar's son Bob, then in his mid-twenties, ran her campaign. (He would continue to be campaign manager, not only for his mother but also for his younger brother Paul, who was the New Democratic MP for Ottawa Centre from 2006 to 2015.)

The *Ottawa Citizen*, which supported Dewar, commented that good local government rather than ideology was the victor: "Although some observers were reading the results as a further incursion of the NDP and left-wingers into municipal politics...the victory Monday was for community-based candidates rather than the informal 'business slate' which did not fare well."[122] When Dewar became mayor she had been a local politician for six years, during which she had become well aware of the complexities of Ottawa's governmental structure.[123] Moreover, although she enjoyed and was committed to local politics – she in fact preferred local to provincial or federal politics – she recognized the limitations of municipal governance. She knew that in Canada, and certainly in Ontario, major decisions would be made not at the local but at the provincial or federal levels.

In spite of these limitations, she did believe that "the mayor of the Capital has a status a regular city mayor doesn't have." "Cities have to talk to cities," she insisted, and not just about sewers and garbage collection, but also about issues like international peace.[124] Dewar would run for mayor again and win in 1980 and 1982. In 1980, as in 1978, her main opponent was Pat Nichol and the campaign was again nasty. In 1982 she ran against Darrel Kent and defeated him.[125] Her supporters consider her to have been a great mayor, and even her enemies believed her to be honest, although they thought that in supporting such causes as disarmament, she was overstepping the boundaries of her local mandate.

Dewar was genuinely committed to thinking globally while acting locally. She was also a shrewd and diligent local politician. She knew that a successful mayor must ensure that municipal services work. She was a success as mayor because she paid close attention to local concerns, but also because she realized the far-reaching effects of using the office to argue for consensus over conflict and discussion over confrontation. Her friend and fellow municipal politician Toddy Kehoe told me that building consensus was Dewar's most important achievement.

Her style of governance was at times quirky. She focused on individuals and she broke rules. Havi Echenberg and Robert Fox, who both worked for Dewar when she was mayor and were both fond of her, each remarked that Dewar's training as a public health nurse shaped her character and her actions. She never stopped thinking like a public health nurse, they both said. Good public health nurses see a problem and they do their best to fix it, right there and then.

Havi Echenberg reminisced about one incident. The mayor's office in the old city hall was huge. One night after hours, Echenberg and Dewar were there together. There was a single lamp lit in the office, creating a small pool of light in the cavernous darkness. The telephone rang. The appropriate thing would have been for Echenberg, as the mayor's assistant, to answer it, rather than the

mayor herself. But Dewar was too quick for her.

Mayor Dewar with two young hockey players. Dewar cared about peace and women's issues, about "thinking globally and acting locally," but she loved meeting with a wide variety of local people, as this photo illustrates.

On the other end of the line was a woman who lived in public housing and who could not pay her gas bill. What did Dewar do? She sent her driver over to the woman's house with a cheque. Echenberg was upset: "Your Worship, you can't help people like that. It doesn't work. There are people who wait days and weeks to get a phone call from you. Lots of people were ahead of her." Dewar's retort was, "Well, I can't help everyone. I helped her."

But Echenberg loved working for the mayor. "With Marion, every day was a fabulous day.... She really was quite remarkably optimistic and energetic." Moreover, Echenberg remarked, she surrounded herself with strong people. She knew that it was important to have people who could say, "You can't do this."

From the time she took office as mayor in 1978 until she stepped down in 1985, Marion Dewar accomplished much, both locally and on the national and international levels. Her commitment to human rights led her to advocate for women, for gays and lesbians, and for First Nations people.[126] She supported peace and disarmament and advocated for openness, multiculturalism, and inclusiveness at the local, national, and international levels.

As mayor she intended to reshape Ottawa's local government. She combated endemic nepotism and she was successful in achieving considerable municipal reform. She improved local policing and she made sure the snow got cleared away. As mayor of Canada's capital, Dewar worked hard to forge alliances and at the same time to resist pressure from the federal government.

As a local politician committed to urban reform, Marion Dewar was not alone. Indeed, in the 1970s and 1980s municipal reform was in the air in urban North America. In other Canadian cities, reforming politicians confronted developers and opposed graft and nepotism. In 1971, Toronto's urban reformers famously succeeded in stopping the Spadina Expressway. (Toronto reformers were not successful when they opposed Ontario Premier Mike Harris's "megacity" in 1998.) There were referenda on peace, not only in Ottawa, but, for example, in Vancouver. However, there were several things that were unique about Marion Dewar. She was the only woman mayor of a large Canadian urban area. Moreover, she was not only a woman, she was a feminist. (Charlotte Hazel McCallion was elected mayor of Mississauga in 1978, but Mississauga was not then an urban area, and McCallion was not a feminist.)

In terms of his ideas and his actions, Toronto urban reformer John Sewell provides a revealing contrast to Dewar. In *Up Against City Hall,* Sewell writes about his fight for municipal reform when he ran for alderman in 1969. His campaign literature stated, "There is a new kind of politics emerging in Canadian cities. It is concerned with changing the way decisions are being made, so that people directly affected by government action – in fields like urban renewal, poverty policies, public housing, planning, tenants' rights – participate in making the decisions involved."[127]

Dewar supported all these causes, but she also advocated for women, whereas Sewell does not appear to have noticed women's issues. Sewell defended public housing tenants, but he, unlike Dewar, never saw their plight as a women's issue.

Rather than attempt to chronicle Dewar's work as mayor in its entirety, I am focusing on a number of specific issues. These include: Project 4000; the cause of peace and disarmament; advocacy for women; support for the arts; and support for the Rideau Centre project.

PROJECT 4000

Project 4000 was the City of Ottawa's plan to welcome 4,000 Southeast Asian refugees – the "boat people" – to the Ottawa community in 1979 and 1980. Countrywide, some 60,000 Southeast Asians settled in Canada during that time,[128] fleeing regimes in Vietnam, Cambodia, and Laos. How and why did this refugee crisis arise? Why was it that some three million Southeast Asians felt it necessary to flee Vietnam, Cambodia, and Laos?

The European invasion of the region in the nineteenth century was crucial. In Southeast Asia, the French gained control over what is today Vietnam, Laos, and Cambodia, colonizing it as French Indochina. During the Second World War, the defeated French lost Indochina. After the end of the war, they struggled to regain their power, but when Dien Bien Phu fell in 1954, they lost it for good.

After the French withdrawal, Vietnam was divided into the North, led by Communist Nationalist Ho Chi Minh, and the South. Gradually, the United States took over from the French, with a war that escalated in the 1960s and early 1970s. But the North defeated the South: on April 30, 1975, the powerful southern capital city of Saigon fell, and the Communist forces gained control, unifying the country, which had always been Ho Chi Minh's objective. In July 1976, Saigon was renamed Ho Chi Minh City.

The people who needed or desperately wanted to leave Vietnam were, first, those who had been directly involved with assisting the United States and, second, those who were actively anti-Communist. If they stayed in Vietnam, these people could expect "re-education" and banishment to a New Economic Zone – not a good thing – or worse.

Then there were the Hoa, or ethnic Chinese minority. This group numbered over 1.3 million people who mainly resided in the South, in or around Saigon. Some of them had lived in Vietnam for generations. Many were small merchants, although some were merchants on a much larger scale. The Hoa had a reputation for being rich. But they, too, suffered a loss of income and status and faced "re-education" and banishment to a New Economic Zone. Vietnamese, both ethnic Vietnamese and Hoa, formed the largest group of Southeast Asian refugees, but there were also refuges from Cambodia and Laos.[129]

Per capita, Canada took in more of these refugees than any other host country. The city of Ottawa came close to the mayor's target of 4,000, and again, per capita, Ottawa took in more refugees than any other Canadian community. This endeavor depended on the remarkable response of hundreds of volunteers from the Ottawa community. It also depended on the good will of the federal government. But above all, it depended on Marion Dewar. It was Dewar who launched Project 4000 in June and July of 1979, and she vigorously promoted it. As NDP activist and provincial politician Evelyn Gigantes remarked to me, "I...remember with awe... the magnificent way she challenged the community and the federal government with her campaign to bring thousands of Vietnamese refugees to Canada, almost all of them people who had supported the American role in Vietnam, which she opposed."

Dewar had advocated for Project 4000 when she was mayor for only a few months. Many believed she rushed into this initiative too quickly. But as she said, "Yes. We could have had more information if we waited. We would have had a better indication if we'd studied the situation for two and a half years, but in the meantime, a lot of people would be at the bottom of the ocean."[130]

The Southeast Asian refugee crisis began in 1975, but it was only in 1978 that it attracted the attention of the media in the non-Asian world. Moreover, although many refugees escaped overland to refugee camps in Thailand, it was the boat people – those who fled in flimsy craft, large or small, braving the treacherous South China Sea – who received media attention.

Mayor Marion Dewar and her husband, Ken, responded to just such media coverage. In June 1979, she and Ken were in the Laurentians, taking a long overdue weekend break. It was raining, so to pass the time, the Dewars started up a game of bridge with another couple. The television was on in the background. All four of them were drawn into what was on the screen: stories about people from Vietnam, fleeing their country in leaky boats, only to be refused landing and even pushed back into the water. In the twenty-first century we are used to seeing distressing events of this kind on television screens or on the Internet. But television images of disaster were still uncommon in 1979. Accordingly, they had a greater impact than they might have now.[131]

Marion Dewar sometimes described herself as ordinary, and indeed, her response to this crisis was that of an average person. She was horrified by the images she saw on television. Her visceral response to the plight of these people is one reason her shock and determination resonated with so many Canadians. She did not subject the media response to the sort of analysis one finds elsewhere. Instead, she acted. And in acting, she was anything but ordinary. She had energy, commitment, and an acute political sense, and as mayor she had power and moral authority. Havi Echenberg, Donna Holtom, and others assert that Dewar made the decision to launch Project 4000 on her own. She consulted Ken, of course. He would always be her most trusted confidant. Her first step was a meeting with community leaders on June 27. She invited religious leaders. She invited Ron Atkey, the federal immigration minister in Prime Minister Joe Clark's newly minted government. She also invited people like Can Le, the dedicated and tireless president of the Vietnamese Community Association, who would later say, "Dewar's political leadership was the key element that moved [Project 4000] forward." Minister Atkey could not come. In his stead, he sent a senior official, who argued that Canada had already done a lot, having just raised the Southeast Asian refugee quota from 4,000 to 8,000. It was at this point, apparently, that Dewar said, "Fine. We'll take the other 4,000." Project 4000 was born.

After the June 27 meeting, Mayor Dewar did consult with her staff and her political allies on city council. They planned for a city council meeting, which would be held on July 4. Dewar knew that it was crucial to obtain the support of council, and at that meeting she was successful in doing so. The council voted for $25,000 of funding for the project.

But she also needed public support. For this, she and her advisors planned a rally to be held at Lansdowne Park on July 12. The meeting proved to be an overwhelming success, although it was a

Mayor Dewar addresses a large and enthusiastic crowd at Lansdowne Park on July 12, 1979. Her subject: Project 4000.

gamble. One reason for its success was careful planning. In June, volunteers were enlisted and goals were formulated.[132] Dewar put her friend and executive assistant Donna Holtom in charge of the rally. But many others were involved, including Dan and Barbara Gamble, the organizers of the successful Christmas Craft Fair. Another reason for the success of the July 12 rally is that Dewar and her project received favourable publicity from the press. The *Ottawa Journal* and the *Ottawa Citizen* both praised the mayor, and both gave advance notice of the rally. The *Journal* editorialized on July 4, 1979, admiring Dewar's "brave initiative." It called the project "the most humanitarian gesture this community has demonstrated in many years."[133] And over the longer term, the consistent and persistent support of Russell Mills, editor of the *Ottawa Citizen*, would prove essential to Project 4000's success. "She convinced me," Mills told me.

The rally was an unforgettable event. Beforehand, devoted and skilled volunteers had set up the hall so that it would seat a few hundred people. They did not want it to look empty.[134] But more

and more people flooded into the Lansdowne space. No one knows how many people came, but it was perhaps as many as 3,000.[135]

Young Vietnamese singers at the Landsdowne rally are singing "O Canada." Their costumes were made by Mrs. Can Le, wife of Ottawa's Vietnamese-Canadian spokesperson.

The program included Alan Breakspear as master of ceremonies. Breakspear was a remarkable humanitarian who was about to take over as the organizer of Project 4000. A group of young Vietnamese singers, organized by Can Le and his wife (she made the girls' costumes), sang "O Canada." Folk singer Bruce Cockburn performed on his guitar. The speakers included Catholic Archbishop Plourde, Anglican Bishop William Robinson, and Rabbi Don Gerber of the new Jewish Reform congregation, Temple Israel, who movingly reminded the audience that the doors had been closed to Jewish refugees after Hitler took power. This must not happen again, Rabbi Gerber insisted. Jewish Canadians responded across the country in greater proportion than their numbers in the population would suggest. Like Rabbi Gerber, Jewish Canadians and their organizations, including the Canadian Jewish Congress, responded by saying, "Not again."[136]

The final speaker was the mayor herself. By all accounts she was inspirational. "The audience rose in a standing ovation of clapping and cheers when Dewar walked to the microphone."[137] After the speeches were over, the crowd, which appears to have been overwhelmingly supportive, surged forward to sign up for volunteer work.

What were they volunteering to do? The 1976 Immigration Act allowed for private as well as government sponsorship of refugees.[138] Project 4000 was designed to facilitate private sponsorship. There is considerable disagreement about whether or not the federal government had to be pushed to take in more refugees from Southeast Asia or whether, in fact, Joe Clark's government took the lead. Flora MacDonald, then Progressive Conservative MP for Kingston and the Islands, served as secretary of state for external affairs in Clark's government. Certainly Flora MacDonald's own memories of her involvement in Project 4000 suggest that the federal government's role was crucial. But others, like Dan Gamble, believed that Marion Dewar was the main mover and shaker: "No government could have contained Marion's determination.... She inspired everyone else."

The success of Project 4000 obscured the fact that there was always strong opposition to the project. Although Vietnamese-Canadian leader Can Le told me that he never met with unpleasant opposition, we do have a record of opponents. The City of Ottawa Archives papers on Project 4000 include a file labeled "Correspondence, Negative." In the file are letters sent to Mayor Dewar, which express fears that the refugees will take jobs away from Canadians and worries about disease.[139] "These people...by numbers alone can and will take over the land from our descendants," wrote one correspondent. Another said the mayor was "losing all sense of judgment...these are not our people, and they are not our responsibility." Paul Dewar remembers hate calls made to his mother at home.[140]

Mayor Dewar's staff and the mayor herself took these letters seriously. In her standard response she said, "Naturally I am disappointed that you do not share my views...but I can assure you the majority of people do."[141]

Marion Dewar doubtless believed this to be the case, but she was in fact wrong. Canada-wide, there was opposition to the Southeast

Asian refugees, and the opposition increased over time rather than diminished.[142] Dewar did everything she could to address this issue. She carefully answered the hostile local correspondence, and she spoke in person and on the radio about generosity, tolerance, and charity. Dewar's openness, her passion, and her commitment to inclusiveness did much to counter opposition, but did not convince everyone.

There were also questions relating to politics and political allegiances. If some people objected to the Southeast Asian refugees because they were xenophobic, others supported the refugees because of their anti-Communist views. Right-wing columnist Barbara Amiel, for example, wrote about "the Asian holocaust" and talked of the "brutal expulsion" carried on by the Vietnamese government and about "genocide."[143] Dewar was, as we've seen, a staunch New Democrat. Barbara Amiel made an unlikely political bedfellow. But Dewar ignored this. What she saw were the drowning, desperate people, rather than the wider politics. The fleeing Southeast Asians needed shelter. That is what she saw and why she acted.

How did Project 4000 operate? One of my informants said of Mayor Dewar, "Marion could delegate." She advocated for the refugees and she was involved in the project, but she knew when to back off. The tight and formal organization of Project 4000 functioned with Dewar playing a background role. Several key people were involved. They included Alan Breakspear (master of ceremonies at the Landsdowne Park rally), who was seconded from his civil service job to manage the project. There was philanthropist Michael Lubbock. And there was Eleanor Ryan, who chaired the executive committee for the project. Vietnamese spokesperson Can Le told me that Ryan not only made policy, she ran Project 4000 on a day-to-day basis.[144]

The work of Project 4000 included, first of all, the organization of sponsoring groups. The law stipulated that individuals could not become sponsors. Instead, groups were formed and each group had to raise a considerable sum of money – $8,000–$12,000 – and had to agree to help the refugee family through its first year. Members met the refugees when they arrived, usually at the Ottawa airport. The group arranged for lodging, food and clothing, language training, job seeking, and medical care. Volunteers were involved at every step.

Clothing was a major challenge. The refugees were coming from a warm climate and would have to face an Ottawa winter. Elizabeth Elton, a volunteer who ran the clothing depot for four months in 1979, was inspired to get involved with Project 4000 when she attended the Lansdowne Park rally. Marion Dewar, she remembers, "was so very compelling." Elizabeth volunteered "on impulse." Elizabeth met me outside 755 Somerset Street West, Ottawa, the same building from which she ran the clothing depot. She brought along a cherished keepsake, a letter from Marion Dewar dated November 14, 1979, thanking her for her volunteer work, which was addressed to her personally as "Liz" and signed "Marion."

Ottawa did become more open to cultural diversity as a result of Project 4000. And Mayor Dewar – through interviews with the media and through direct action – did all she could to make sure that the image of the Vietnamese was a good one.

If the refugees changed Ottawa, at least to some degree, how was it for them? Being a refugee may be lifesaving, but it is hard and sad. Yes, the Southeast Asian refugees were exemplary new Canadians. As Russell Mills commented, "They were good people: hardworking, family oriented people, who did not get into trouble." However, many members of the first generation suffered deeply. A minority of Southeast Asian refugees did get depressed and some committed suicide. There was some family violence and there were even murders.[145]

Language acquisition, the research suggests, was important to success. Learning a second language was easier for the refugees who came from urban areas and were literate in their own language. But even then there were difficulties. One of my interviewees, Lynne Young – at the time an ESL instructor, but now a professor of linguistics and language studies at Carleton University – volunteered for Project 4000. She told me that although Ottawa's language acquisition program was clearly well-intentioned, it had many flaws, and for many of the refugees, it was inadequate.

Finding appropriate work was another challenge. Getting work of some sort was possible. Thirty per cent of the refugees had found jobs within a month of arrival. But they often did not find jobs commensurate with their previous training and experience, especially if that had been extensive.[146] As a result, the first generation was inclined to put its faith in the second generation, many of whom did succeed.

Most of the Vietnamese boat people were indeed from Vietnam, although there were also significant numbers from Laos and Cambodia. And the Vietnamese were not all from the same background. Many people, even many of the Project 4000 volunteers, did not realize that in Ottawa, of the Vietnamese who came, just over half were ethnic Chinese. The ethnic Chinese did receive extensive help from existing Chinese organizations here in Canada, but they also sometimes experienced prejudice and hostility from the older Chinese community.[147]

With Project 4000, Mayor Dewar meant to do more than rescue the boat people. It was part of a wider effort to create a more open and caring civic culture. As Donna Holtom commented, Dewar believed in "fairness and in inclusion." She wanted to "change the culture." And she was deeply committed to "diversity." To this end, she reached out to francophones and she built relationships with Ottawa's various ethnic communities.

MAYOR DEWAR AND THE CAUSE OF PEACE

"I hope I die an idealist. You have to have goals, values, and objectives. How else would you get up in the morning?"[148] Marion Dewar made that comment to journalist Barbara Freeman in a 1985 interview focusing on the mayor and the peace movement.

Dewar cared deeply about the cause of world peace, and as mayor she used her moral and political power to advocate for it. As Robert Fox said of her, war "was a violation of her faith, an obscene distortion."

"I have always been a strong proponent of global change through local action," Dewar said in her inaugural address of 1982. To that end she successfully supported a referendum on nuclear disarmament that was held in conjunction with the municipal election of November 1982. Seventy-seven per cent of the voters who turned out supported this referendum. As Dewar liked to remind audiences, this was the first such referendum held in Canada.[149]

Following the success of the disarmament referendum, Mayor

Mayor Dewar in Grenada, in 1983,
protesting the American invasion.
That action took courage.

Dewar brought a resolution to Ottawa City Council calling for the city to declare itself a "nuclear weapons free zone."[150] Although the resolution failed to attain a majority in Council, introducing it was not a failure, she told Barbara Freeman, because it fostered discussion. Dewar firmly believed that grassroots public discussion was essential if public opinion on disarmament was to change: "When citizens talk about peace, they are dismissed as being naïve and ignorant. When doctors and scientists speak of the horrendous results of nuclear confrontation, they too are dismissed as being naïve. National governments have perfected the art of disempowering those who oppose the arms race."[151]

Dewar's actions as mayor in support of peace and nonviolence included writing the head of the National Research Council (NRC) to oppose research on chemical weapons. The NRC, she told its president, "has been carrying on experimentations which could be used for the purposes of germ warfare. Your immediate response to this inquiry would be most appreciated as well as a full disclosure...."[152] As mayor, she expressed her official disapproval of Canada's decision to abstain on a United Nations resolution denouncing the American invasion of Grenada, and she went to Grenada herself.[153] She also participated in a large "Refuse the Cruise" demonstration held in Ottawa on October 30, 1982. Ten thousand people came to this rally. Mayor Dewar's presence added weight to the rally and encouraged the participants.

Peace historian Thomas Socknat commented about the Refuse the Cruise campaign:

> Since the Vietnam War had diverted Canadians from the nuclear arms build-up, popular interest in disarmament only revived in 1979 when NATO responded to the Soviet build-up of medium-range nuclear missiles with plans to station Cruise and Pershing II missiles in Europe. Mass demonstrations erupted across Europe and in Canada protest rallies drew record numbers.... But it was American plans to test the Cruise missiles in Canada that resulted in a mushrooming of peace groups across the country in the "Refuse the Cruise" campaign.[154]

The culmination of Dewar's struggles for peace during her mayoralty came in 1985, on the fortieth anniversary of the dropping of two

Buttons, including one for the October 30, 1982 "Refuse the Cruise" rally. I was at that rally. It was unforgettable.

atomic bombs by the United States on the Japanese cities of Hiroshima and Nagasaki. In August 1985, she went to Hiroshima for a conference of mayors: "At the conference there was the intangible feeling of solidarity and strength...we pledged ourselves to transcend the barriers of race, government, culture, and creed to...secure against nuclear destruction...."[155]

The North American peace movement of the 1960s continued into the 1980s, fuelled by a fear of nuclear war and contamination by radioactivity.[156] Many people loved Marion Dewar for her staunch support of peace, but not everyone approved. In November 1983, she received a letter from an outraged constituent: "I am embarrassed by you making a fool of yourself when you are on the podium with do-gooder peacenik radicals of the world.... Marion we did not elect you...to be part of a 'world political forum.' The U.S. is the only thing that stands between us and world communist domination."[157]

When writer Clive Doucet, who would later enter city politics himself, wrote:

"I...heard our mayor speak on the subject of disarmament. I was so proud to be in the crowd...and grateful to live in a city that had such a mayor," Dewar sent him this answer: "I have received many letters and calls accusing me of being in with the Communists, and worse, and your letter is heartening and refreshing...."[158]

Dewar's advocacy of peace raises important questions. What is the scope of municipal government? Should it include advocacy for disarmament? Dewar was convinced that it must: "As a strong believer in disarmament, a municipal administrator who knows that if anything is left after a nuclear holocaust the city will have to clean it up, and, as an individual who is sufficiently well informed to know that cities will be the target of such an attack, I am convinced that this question is a 'municipal question.'"[159]

Dewar's position was that a mayor must and inevitably will engage with political issues. Advocacy was part of the job. But she also struggled to achieve consensus. Although Dewar did not wish to acknowledge them, there are tensions between advocacy and consensus. Anyone who supports peace and disarmament and the "think globally, act locally" policies that Dewar advocated as mayor would most likely have supported her. But a peace advocate (like me) would most likely not have supported a right-wing mayor who had no use for the arts, was a booster for arms manufacturers, opposed public housing, and was anti-feminist. And right-wingers did not support Mayor Dewar.

Dewar did believe deeply in working for consensus, questioning the views of "experts," and encouraging grassroots activism. But she never wanted to force her beliefs on anyone. Instead, she worked for patient and persistent persuasion. Did she believe that her support for consensus arose from the fact that she was a woman? Did she believe in a "feminist peace politics," as it has been articulated, for example, by theorist Sarah Ruddick?

> This politics expresses a sturdy suspicion of organized violence even in the best of causes. Accordingly, it seeks to expose the multiple costs of violence and to disrupt the plans of those who organize it.... A feminist peace politics contributes in distinctively feminist ways to the threefold aim of fomenting sturdy suspicion of organized violence, disclosing hidden violence, and inventing the strategies and ideals of nonviolence.[160]

These words could be seen as a summation of the ways that Marion Dewar worked for peace. She did believe that peace was

Mayor Dewar meets with Chairman Mao on one of her trips to China.

a grassroots issue. She did believe that co-op-eration, understanding, and discussion would lead people to accept nuclear disarmament and the way of peace. She did have a "sturdy suspicion" of the use of violence. Moreover, she was identified, and identified herself, as a feminist peace activist.

However, I have found no evidence that during her years in local politics Dewar read theoretical works on feminism and peace. Marion was a doer, not an abstract thinker. She exemplifies what Ruddick and others express, but she did not derive her views from reading Ruddick. She appears in Bonnie Sher Klein's film, *Speaking Our Peace,* with Ursula Franklin, one of the most erudite of Canadian feminist peace activists.[161] But it does not appear that Franklin's ideas influenced her. She just went ahead and did what she felt morally compelled to do.

Did she believe that women were more inclined to support peace and co-operation than men? She did, although she believed that such differences were rooted in culture, not in biology. As she told Barbara Freeman in 1985, women were raised in a culture of caring, and this was enough to explain their commitment to peace and consensus.

ADVOCACY FOR WOMEN

Since girlhood, Marion Dewar had been an advocate for girls and women. Her father's refusal to pay for her education at Queen's University, where she would have studied science, most likely fuelled and focused her beliefs about the injustices women faced and the rights women should have. True, she did go into nursing, a classic "woman's profession." She may not have been enthusiastic at first, but she came to love nursing as a skilled and caring profession. Moreover, she came to believe that caring included the responsibility to care for the world.

Caring, co-operation, acting locally and thinking globally: not only were these qualities of prime importance to Dewar, she believed that women were more capable of advancing them than men. During her political life, women's rights were always part of her agenda. She supported all sorts of socially conscious groups, including, for example, the charity Causeway, which helps both men and women with mental illness,[162] but she did make a point of supporting individual women and feminist groups.

She supported and encouraged women involved in politics. She was close to Evelyn Gigantes, who had a long and mostly successful career as an NDP politician at the provincial level. The two women carried on a warm correspondence. Dewar vigorously supported Gigantes in 1981, when she ran and lost at the provincial level, and Ottawa's French-language newspaper *Le Droit* criticized Gigantes for attempting to combine politics with motherhood. (She had run when she was pregnant with her second child.) Dewar defended Gigantes vociferously.[163] Evelyn Gigantes was well known, but Dewar also encouraged women who were not well known. In 1985, she tried to persuade one such Ottawa woman to run for alderman. The woman decided against running, largely because her husband was opposed.[164] Finally, Dewar supported explicitly feminist organizations such as the Women's Career Counselling Centre and the Ottawa Women's Bookstore.[165]

As mayor, Dewar did advocate specifically and directly for women and for feminism. I examine two issues in which she

Mayor Dewar marches with supporters of the Ottawa Women's Credit Union. Dewar is in the front, to the left. Dewar was indeed a woman of action.

was involved. One transcends local, provincial, national, and international boundaries, namely her support for the grassroots movement to promote what became Section 28 of the Canadian Charter of Rights and Freedoms. The second issue, a local one, involves her vigorous support for the appointment of Maude Barlow as Ottawa's Equal Opportunity Officer.

"THE TAKING OF TWENTY-EIGHT"[166]

"We had, right on the floor of this office, babies that were sleeping and mothers that were breastfeeding."[167] That was Marion Dewar's 1985 recollection of one of her actions, in February 1981, in support of what became known as the Ad Hoc Conference, advocating for extended rights for women in the Canadian Charter of Rights and

Freedoms. Section 28 reads as follows: "Notwithstanding anything in this Charter, the rights and freedoms referred to in it are guaranteed equally to male and female persons."

When the 1982 Constitution Act was passed, the Charter contained Section 28. The story of how "Twenty-Eight" came to be is a complicated one, about which feminist historians and activists disagree. There is no doubt that it involved Lloyd Axworthy, who, in addition to being minister of employment and immigration in Pierre Trudeau's second government, was also minister responsible for the status of women. Axworthy clashed with Doris Anderson, then head of the Canadian Advisory Council on the Status of Women, and in the course of her disputes with Minister Axworthy, Anderson resigned.

Many believe that Pierre Trudeau could have done better than appoint Axworthy as the minister responsible for the status of women. According to some, Axworthy had a limited understanding of women's issues. Some women remember his patronizing remarks and his irritability.[168] According to Anderson, the specific issue precipitating her resignation was Axworthy's insistence on the cancellation of a conference that was to have been sponsored by the advisory council. Most of the advisory council members, loyal Liberals, supported the minister. But Doris Anderson said, "Every time Lloyd Axworthy opens his mouth, one hundred more women become feminists."[169]

After Anderson's resignation and the cancellation of the conference, women's groups throughout the country very quickly planned the Ad Hoc Conference, to be held at the same time (Feb. 14–15, 1981) and place (Ottawa) as the cancelled conference.

Some 1,300 women came to the conference, and hundreds of Ottawa women helped to house them. As we have seen, Mayor Dewar, who opened up city hall to the conference participants, was one of them. On February 15, the second day of the Ad Hoc Conference, the group met at city hall and the meeting ended with a rousing speech from Dewar herself. As she told Debra Pilon of *Herizons*, the fight for women's Charter rights was "a highlight of her term as mayor."[170]

Dewar was taking considerable risks with this advocacy. It took courage and a deep sense of commitment for the mayor of Ottawa to run up against the governing federal Liberals. Why did she do it?

The evidence is scant, but we can surmise that it stemmed, at least in part, from her membership in the New Democratic Party and her close association with NDP MP Pauline Jewett, who supported what became Section 28 of the Charter of Rights and Freedoms. NDP MP Margaret Mitchell, who, like Jewett, supported Section 28, may also have had an influence on Dewar.[171]

EQUAL OPPORTUNITY AT CITY HALL

As mayor, Dewar's most important internal initiative in support of women was her strong advocacy of the appointment of Maude Barlow as director of the Office of Equal Opportunity for the City of Ottawa. This was an important and difficult initiative, one that took considerable courage. The city's Office of Equal Opportunity was created in 1976, well before Dewar's mayoralty, but in its early years the director's position was precarious – it had little visibility, and opposition to the creation of the office within city management was intense: "There should be no preference for male or female and a special drive to attract women is not justified," said one department head.[172]

As Evelyn Gigantes told me, "When Marion brought Maude Barlow to city hall, it was like a breath of fresh air." Barlow's appointment did represent a radical change. Barlow became director of equal opportunity for the city in 1980, serving for three years. She was recommended for appointment by a committee that included Alderman Kehoe, who at one point in the procedure "expressed great concern relative to the general inaction of the program over the last five years."[173] The committee met several times over the summer of 1980 and considered several candidates. At its in camera meeting of June 25, 1980, the committee recommended the appointment of Maude Barlow. She took office in September 1980.[174]

Did the city know what it was getting when it hired Maude Barlow? Probably not. The prominence she has garnered since the 1980s certainly testifies to her courage, skill, and tenacity as an advocate for a wide range of causes, including the integrity of the Canadian press and most recently for people's right, worldwide, to clean water.[175] But her appointment to the city post, when she was thirty-three, was her first real public challenge. It was a breakthrough for her, as well as for the city. Barlow, who married at nineteen, was, in her own words, a "sweet little housewife." But in the early 1970s, she discovered feminism, reading Andrea Dworkin and Germaine Greer.

From the time she took office, Maude Barlow was determined to give feminist views and feminist policies a high profile at city hall. And so was Mayor Dewar. Barlow herself says that she was able to be so effective because she had Dewar's support. During her three years at the city, Barlow told me, "We did a lot." Marion Dewar "really meant it" and during those years progress was made with the police, firefighters, and road workers. "Marion stood by me," Maude says. But it was "no picnic at city hall." There were "no proper procedures for hiring or firing. There were no sexual harassment procedures." Much of the city's workforce was not only male and blue-collar, but managers "didn't take kindly to someone advocating fair play for women – or men. They'd done it in a traditional 'you hire my nephew and I'll hire yours' way and they didn't want to change." In short, nepotism was endemic and widely accepted.

Soon after she took office, Barlow launched a series of brown bag lunches on controversial topics relating to women and equal opportunity. These were truly radical events, disturbing to many people, but Mayor Dewar was ready and willing to defend her equal opportunity officer. Lawyer and legal historian Constance Backhouse was the speaker at one such meeting, held on March 20, 1981. Backhouse has vivid memories of this occasion. She recalls that Barlow, whom she met for the first time that day was…

> wonderful – astute, charismatic and inspiring…over breakfast, she had fully coached me on the gender politics of the event. Sexual harassment was a huge problem within the city's work-force. Some of the women who would be seated in the audience had suffered personally from unwanted sexual overtures. Among the men would be some of the city's most tenacious and flagrant perpetrators, who had been told that their attendance at the workshop was mandatory. They would be sitting in the front rows, arms crossed in defiance, ready for a fight.

Maude Barlow's prediction was accurate. Today, most Canadian employers and employees are familiar with the term "sexual harass-ment." Three decades ago, this was not the case. Barlow, who was indeed astute and who had done her homework, asked Backhouse because, along with Leah Cohen, Backhouse was a pioneer in recognizing, uncovering, labelling, and publicizing the phenomenon of unwanted workplace sexual advances.[176]

The mayor was a staunch supporter of Barlow and her uncompromising approach. In return, Barlow became an enthusiastic champion of Dewar. As Barlow told Dewar in January 1982, "This last year has been one of the most productive and pleasant of my life. I thank you for the opportunity."[177] Dewar's support for Barlow's radical work appears to have been unique in Canada, but, like many feminist achievements, it has been largely ignored. Unless they were feminists themselves, those who wrote about municipal reform in Canada in the 1970s and 1980s had little to say about feminism, or indeed about women. But Dewar's achievement deserves to be celebrated.

THE ARTS

Well before Marion Dewar became mayor, the acerbic journalist Alan Fotheringham famously dubbed Ottawa "coma city."[178] During her years as a local politician, Marion Dewar did all she could to change Ottawa from a dull, civil service town into a community with a plethora of ethnic restaurants, fairs, local theatres, and galleries.

Ottawa in the 1980s was not Montreal, Vancouver, or Toronto, nor is it today. The three most populous Canadian metropolitan centres have large arts communities. Writers, musicians, and filmmakers, not surprisingly, gravitate to these big cities. Ottawa has never had the same drawing power. However, there have always been writers, musicians, and visual artists in Ottawa, and some of them have promoted and fought for the local arts community. One such person is Arthur Milner, who was for many years involved with the Great Canadian Theatre Company. In the 1970s Milner was president of the Ottawa-Carleton Arts Coalition. Its resounding slogan was, "Culture is not the icing on the cake, it is the cake."[179] During her mayoralty, Dewar strove to give this point of view genuine meaning.

The history of Ottawa's local arts community is intertwined with the city's position as the federal capital. The federal presence interacted – as it continues to interact – with the local arts community, sometimes to its benefit and sometimes to its detriment. Although the National Arts Centre was launched in 1966 by Lester Pearson, it was Pierre Trudeau who had a vision for the National Arts Centre, and he was prime minister when it officially opened in 1969. The federal presence, through the National Arts Centre, did make an enormous difference. The city had been without a proper performing arts hall for more than thirty years, and the building itself made an important contribution. Moreover, the National Arts Centre brought people to Ottawa – most notably the musicians who joined the National Arts Centre Orchestra – who settled here and became part of the local arts community as teachers and performers.

Dewar was never opposed to the federal presence on the arts scene. Indeed, she did all she could to have her voice and the city's voice heard as supporters. What she wanted was a strong local presence that would complement the federal institutions. She supported the arts as alderman, as a member of the Board of Control, and as mayor. As mayor she acted in direct and personal ways. She bought art for the city, including, for example, a Benjamin Chee-Chee painting.[180]

As with all aspects of her work as mayor, Dewar was especially concerned with supporting women, as she did when she bought the "The Company of Artists and Patrons" portfolio in 1983, a project initiated by artist Susan Geraldine Taylor.[181] Not all the artists included in Taylor's portfolio were women, but most were. Years later, when I interviewed Taylor, along with artist Jerry Grey, both had only positive things to say about Dewar: She "opened all the doors," she "opened her mayoral suite. She really believed in the arts."

Jerry Grey was the artist selected in 1982 to create a large mosaic mural for the new Ottawa police station on Elgin Street.[182] That mural is there because of Marion Dewar. Both Jerry Grey and Susan Taylor remembered that when work on the mosaic was in progress, and Grey and others – like Taylor – were working long hours to complete it, Mayor Dewar came in late one night to cheer them on.

The police station itself – not just the mural – is also there because of Mayor Dewar. There are two plaques in the main hall commemorating the opening of the building by the Prince and Princess of Wales in June 1983. Dewar knew that the prince and princess would be there, and of course she would be there too, as mayor. She wore an elegant blue dress for the occasion. Robert Fox recalls that the dress was custom-made: "She did not buy it at Carlingwood Mall," he said. Carlingwood Mall is a low-key suburban shopping centre near the Dewars' house on Rex Avenue. Marion Dewar – who had little interest in clothes, although she did try to "dress the part" when she was mayor – usually did her shopping there.

Dewar, as an individual and as mayor, was a backer of the Great Canadian Theatre Company. She supported Theatre Ballet of Canada, an Ottawa group. Many in the arts community admired and loved her. They included notable Ottawa painter Morton Baslaw, who wrote to her in 1984 to say, "I am one of your biggest fans."[183]

On a broader and more official scale, Dewar initiated two ventures as mayor. The first was the Mayor's Advisory Group on Arts and Culture (MAG).[184] The advisory group, which met for the first time on March 18, 1980, comprised a number of Ottawa luminaries in the arts world, including music patron Trudi le Caine, folk music promoters Harvey and Louise Glatt, Arthur Milner, visual artist Pat Durr, and English professor, writer, and critic Tom Henighan. Robert Fox was the advisor from the mayor's staff and his services proved to be invaluable.

Tom Henighan was hired to write the MAG final report, which appeared in September 1980. Henighan had taught in the Department of English at Carleton University since 1965. He was invited to join the Mayor's Advisory Group because in the 1970s and 1980s he was not only teaching at Carleton, he was writing regularly for *The Penny Press* (later the *Ottawa Revue*) which was, Henighan recollects, an "arts powerhouse...a focal point for the Ottawa arts community. It was artist-centred and quite different from the *Citizen*. We reviewed almost everything and had strong contacts with the arts community. We were very well known and mostly respected." (Henighan's career as a writer began later, and since his retirement from Carleton, it has flourished.) He was also arts commentator for the morning show on the television station CJOH. He was, in short, a person to be reckoned with on the Ottawa arts scene.

The final report's "Major Recommendations and Suggested Implementation" included advocacy for an Ottawa-Carleton arts council and support for the founding and financing of an Ottawa centre for the visual and performing arts. The Mayor's Advisory Group members had discussed at length the effect of the federal presence on local artists. The 1980 report trenchantly takes on this issue:

> Why should the local artist expect the city and region to create their own arts policies, given the complex federal and provincial support structures already in place? The answer is very simple. Historically, and up to the present day, the city has been a social unit closely associated with the most vigorous artistic and cultural expression…the city is much more tangible and real to the artist than a national or provincial bureau or department.[185]

On the establishment of an Ottawa centre for the visual and performing arts, the report strongly recommended that the old Ottawa Teachers' College building at 195 Elgin Street be selected as this space.

When I interviewed him thirty years later, Henighan, who has vivid memories of his work in the arts community in the 1970s and 1980s, told me that while the National Arts Centre was a boon for Ottawa, it was also a problem. The people who ran the National Arts Centre were, he says, part of the Liberal party's "cultural circle… and local artists were not part of the Liberal vision…" For example, Donald MacSween, who ran the National Arts Centre, was focused on international rather than local artists.

While Mayor Dewar could launch her advisory group on the arts, obtaining funding for its recommendations was another matter altogether. City council did support many of the final report's recommendations, but the regional council did not. As the Reeve of Gouldburn Township said, "It's another example of the region subsidizing Ottawa."[186]

The final report also ran into opposition from members of the public who, unlike the Reeve of Gouldburn Township, opposed Henighan's report because they believed it did not go far enough. They expressed their views at a public meeting held at the Glebe Community Centre on October 29, 1980. Some two hundred people attended this meeting and its minutes record support for grassroots artists. "The emphasis in the Henighan report is on providing large scale facilities…for established organizations…. Ultimately it is the unknown emerging artist who most requires encouragement…."[187]

The report's recommendations did lead to Mayor Dewar's second big effort on behalf of the arts community: her attempt to get funding for an Ottawa centre for the visual and performing arts, using the old teachers' college building. This did not come to pass. In spite of this failure, it is clear that Dewar was a mayor who really cared about the arts. As Tom Henighan puts it, "Under the Dewar administration those of us interested in the arts, and wanting to create a more communal and culturally resonant city, always felt we had a sympathetic ear at City Hall."

DEVELOPMENT AND THE RIDEAU CENTRE

When I asked Donna Holtom, chief of staff during Dewar's first term, what Dewar's greatest achievement as mayor was, she replied, "One that probably hasn't been mentioned yet: the Rideau Centre." Ottawa's Rideau Centre is a large indoor shopping mall, constructed in the early 1980s during Dewar's mayoralty. Its outstanding feature is that it is a downtown rather than a suburban mall, and everyone involved expressed support for the idea that it was designed to revitalize Ottawa's shabby downtown core.

As controller and deputy mayor, Marion Dewar supported the Rideau Centre project, and as mayor she shepherded it into being. Many of her supporters assumed she would oppose it. She was known, after all, for her opposition to growth for the sake of growth. She received a letter from one such supporter in May 1978: "Can't you put a stop to this Rideau Centre idiocy?...Who needs all this Rideau development.... There are shopping centres sprouting up all over the city and taking away the trade from the small businesses that really serve the needs of local people, as with the Bank St. stores."[188] Dewar was forthright in her reply to this correspondent: "I am not in agreement with your opposition to the Rideau Centre project. We really do have to keep our downtown vital and it seems to be one way it could be done."

When I interviewed Ottawa architect Barry Padolsky, he told me that Marion Dewar was correct. The Rideau Centre plan was "an attempt to revitalize downtown Ottawa." From its inception, the project generated conflict. According to Padolsky, Ottawa's downtown core certainly did need revitalizing. The question was, how might this best be achieved? Padolsky points out that there was a more general problem, common to many cities across North America in the decades after the Second World War. "The downtowns were dying." There was a "flight to the suburbs." The old centres, the downtown cores, were being "hollowed out."

Padolsky and like-minded individuals and groups wanted a comprehensive plan that would include private and subsidized housing in the downtown core, a sensible plan for automobile and commercial traffic and for public transit, and a determination to preserve areas that were part of Ottawa's local heritage, most notably the Byward Market, founded in 1827, one of the oldest, continuously thriving food and flower markets in Canada.

And so Padolsky found himself leading the opposition to the plan approved by Ottawa City Council in October 1978. The council approved the "transit mall" (also known as the "bus mall") for Rideau Street. Padolsky was the spokesperson for the Rideau Street Public Advisory Committee. In that capacity he sent a letter to all members of the regional council, in which he explained that they should be aware of "the unanimous, overwhelming and publically recorded opposition of all the downtown citizens' groups and business groups to this proposal." He called it a "lackluster, economically stillborn, and publically unpopular scheme." He also noted that there was a need to save the "unique" Byward Market area.[189]

In the summer of 1978, Padolsky had met with Dewar, who had "then promised me that there would be no bus mall...I had great respect for Marion...but she broke that promise." Padolsky told me it was a failure, in part, because it never became the light-filled, plant-filled "galleria" some had envisioned: "The transit mall...will feature wide sidewalks, extensive landscaping, a pedestrian mall on William Street, covered bus stops and, possibly, enclosed sidewalks." This urban streetscape – which could have been beautiful and would have enhanced Ottawa's downtown – never came into being, because of its cost.[190] Instead, the Rideau Street mall that was constructed quickly became dirty, smelly, and frequented by homeless people. (It was, at least, warmer in winter than the exposed streets.) Barry Padolsky publically denounced what it had become, and it was his firm that removed it in the early 1990s.

The old Rideau Street was transformed in the wake of the coming of the Rideau Centre, which saw completion in 1982.

The five locally owned department stores disappeared. However, although there were dire predictions about the death of the Byward Market, the market has thrived into the twenty-first century and the Rideau Centre bustles with shoppers.

Still, questions remain: Why did Marion Dewar put so much energy into support for a shopping centre, and why did she support the transit mall? Barry Padolsky believes she did so because she was genuinely convinced that Ottawa's downtown had to be revitalized and she was dismayed by the seeming paralysis that had overcome the discussion. The players – business, the community groups, the city, and the region – had all been talking since 1972, but nothing had happened. Something had to be done.

Furthermore, Padolsky commented, the unions representing the building trades were at odds with the community groups. They wanted this massive project because it would provide jobs for their members. Moreover, Dewar did believe that part of her mandate as mayor involved support for the business community. That support was most assuredly expressed through her voice as mayor in favour of the Rideau Centre.

CONCLUSION

As alderman, controller, and mayor, Dewar fought for and deeply believed in progressive causes. These included peace, women's rights, social programs, and a commitment to a public spirit of co-operation and generosity. In the 1960s, the decade in which Dewar's political views were formed, and in the early 1970s, when she entered public life, progressive ideas flourished. But by the 1980s attitudes were changing. Margaret Thatcher became prime minister of the United Kingdom in 1979, Ronald Reagan was elected president of the United States in 1980, and Brian Mulroney became prime minister of Canada in 1984. A "conservative revolution" had begun.[191] The period 1972–1985 was an ideal time for Marion Dewar to do her work as a local politician. By 1985, those progressive times were fading fast.

ENDNOTES:

[122] "Voting Day at a Glance," *Ottawa Citizen*, November 14, 1978, 1 and 8. Nichol was a woman, but she was not an advocate for women. The total number of votes cast was 95,448.

[123] See Andrew (1983), 140–165.

[124] City of Ottawa Archives, Marion Dewar Fonds, A2010-0766, folder 9. Notes written by Dewar: "Thoughts on returning from The Hague" 8/2/1984.

[125] Terms for mayor of Ottawa and municipal elections were one year until 1940; two years from 1940–1982; and three years starting in 1985.

[126] City of Ottawa Archives, Marion Dewar Fonds, A 2010 0766, folder 16. On gays and lesbians, for example, see letter written in 1988 to Dewar, from Gretchen Hartly of Duncan, BC. "One of my coworkers...told me...of the memory she has of you speaking at...the first Gay and Lesbian Conference...She was very impressed, particularly because she'd heard that you'd received at least 50 letters demanding that you not support this conference. You inspire us all!"

[127] Sewell, 53. Much of the literature on municipal reform says little or nothing about women or feminism: *Municipal Reform in Canada: Reconfiguration, Re-Empowerment, and Rebalancing,* Joseph Garcea and Edward C. LeSage Jr, eds., (Toronto: Oxford University Press, 2005) has an article on Ontario by David Siegel, "Municipal Reform in Ontario: Revolutionary Evolution," 127–148, which, like the others in the book, deals primarily with the 1990s, and it briefly discusses the 1970s, but says nothing about women – although the book's cover features a photo with Mayor Barbara Hall front and centre, protesting the "megacity"; *Urban Governance in Canada: Representation, Resources, and Restructuring,* Katherine A. Graham, Susan D. Phillips, with Allan M. Maslove, (Toronto: Harcourt Canada, 1998) says something about women but not much; *Urban Political Systems: A Functional Analysis of Metro Toronto,* Harold Kaplan, (1967) says nothing about women or feminist issues, and Kaplan refers to councilors as "men." One could expect more, even in 1967.

[128] Brian Buckley, *Gift of Freedom: How Ottawa Welcomed the Vietnamese, Cambodian, and Laotian Refugees* (Renfrew, ON: General Store Publishing House, 2008), 27. See also Howard Adelman, *Canada and the Indochinese Refugees* (Regina: L.A. Weigl Educational Associates Ltd., 1982), 23 and passim. Adelman was a key figure in Toronto's "Operation Lifeline" and a York University professor. See also Bruce Grant, *The Boat People: An 'Age' Investigation* (Harmondsworth, England: Penguin, 1979) for a world-wide overview.

[129] For more information on this vast subject see *Southeast Asian Exodus: From Tradition to Resettlement,* Elliott Tepper ed., (Ottawa: Canadian Asian Studies Association 1980); See also Adelman, and Buckley.

[130] Buckley, 32.

[131] At least there is a general perception that this is the case. For an analysis, see Ron Steinman, *Inside Television's First War,* (Columbia, MO: University of Missouri Press, 2002).

[132] City of Ottawa Archives, papers on Project 4000, MG 013.

[133] *Ottawa Journal*, July 4, 1979; from a clipping book lent to me by Can Le.

[134] These skilled volunteers included Barb and Dan Gamble and Sue and George Pike. See Buckley (2008), 88, for references to his interviews with them.

[135] Buckley, 37.

[136] Adelman, 127.

[137] Buckley, 39–40.

[138] See essays in Tepper, ed. (1980).

[139] City of Ottawa Archives, Marion Dewar Fonds, A 2008–0699, "Correspondence Negative" 1-1-(5).

[140] Paul Dewar, CBC "Ottawa Morning," June 19, 2014.

[141] City of Ottawa Archives, Marion Dewar Fonds, A 2008-0699, "Correspondence Negative" 1-1-(5). See letter to Stewart Crawford, dated 8/21/1979.

[142] Adelman, 1–3 and passim.

[143] Barbara Amiel, "Now an Asian Holocaust?" *Maclean's*, July 2, 1979. Clipping in City of Ottawa Archives, Project 4000, 0699 1-1-1.

[144] Within months after the formation of the board of directors, Ryan became chair of Project 4000's executive committee. "I was able to do it because of my work," she said, referring to her extensive experience in the public service and the trade union movement. Eleanor Ryan generously allowed me access to her extensive collection of papers relating to Project 4000.

[145] See Penny van Esterik, "Cultural Factors," in Tepper, ed.; Morton Beiser, *Strangers at the Gate: The "Boat People's" First Ten Years in Canada* (Toronto: University of Toronto Press, 1999), "Migration is a risk for developing mental disorder..." 8. See unpublished report by Gertrud Neuwirth and John Harp "Civic Sponsorship and Southeast Asian Refugees" n.d. but 1979, City of Ottawa Archives, A2008-0700, on Project 4000.

[146] Neuwirth and Harp typescript, v–vi: "Thirty per cent of the respondents began working within one month of arriving...[but the] ability to transfer one's previous occupational skills...takes about three to four years to accomplish, if it is accomplished at all."

[147] See Lawrence Lam, *From Being Uprooted to Surviving: Resettlement of Vietnamese-Chinese "Boat People" in Montreal, 1980-1990* (Toronto: York Lane Press, 1996).

[148] From an interview with Marion Dewar conducted by journalist (later Carleton professor) Barbara Freeman. "Marion Dewar on Peace, October 30, 1985."

[149] Editorial, *Ottawa Citizen*, November 9, 1982, 8.

[150] City of Ottawa Archives, Marion Dewar Fonds, Box 2, folder 10.

[151] City of Ottawa Archives, Marion Dewar Fonds, A2010-0767, "Speeches 1985," "Health Professionals for Nuclear Responsibility."

[152] City of Ottawa Archives, Marion Dewar Fonds, folder 3. Letter of March 4, 1980 from Dewar as mayor to Dr. W. G. Schneider president of NRC.

[153] City of Ottawa Archives, Marion Dewar Fonds, 2010 0765 Box 1, Folder 7 1984, January–June 1984. See Dewar's letter to External Affairs Minister Allan MacEachern, 2/23/1984.

[154] Thomas Socnat, "Conscientious Objectors in the Context of Canadian Peace Movements," *Journal of Mennonite Studies*, vol. 25 (2007) 61–74, 69–70.

[155] City of Ottawa Archives, Marion Dewar Fonds, A2010-0767, "Speeches 1985," "Health Professionals for Nuclear Responsibility."

[156] Tarah Brookfield, *Cold War Comforts: Canadian Women, Child Safety, and Global Insecurity, 1945-1975* (Waterloo, ON: Wilfrid Laurier University Press, 1912). For an overview with a Canadian focus, see especially ch. 3.

[157] City of Ottawa Archives, Marion Dewar Fonds, Correspondence, 1983, folder 6, Letter from Rev. Bob Taylor, 22/22/1983.

[158] City of Ottawa Archives, Marion Dewar Fonds, Box 1, folder 6. Ducet to Dewar, n.d. but 11/28/1983 stamp. Her reply is 11/17/1983.

[159] City of Ottawa Archives, Marion Dewar Fonds, A 2010 0765 box 1, folder 7, 1984. 1984 draft of Dewar's review of a book by Patrick Boyer.

[160] Sara Ruddick, "Towards a Feminist Peace Politics," in *Gendering War Talk*, Miriam Cooke and Angela Woollacott, eds., (Princeton: Princeton University Press, 1993), 109. Among an extensive collection of books that theorize these questions, see also: *Women, Militarism and War*, Jean Bethke Elshtain & Sheila Tobias, eds., (Savage, MD.: Rowman & Littlefield, 1990) and Margaret Higonnet & Jane Jenson, eds., *Behind the Lines* (New Haven: Yale University Press, 1987).

[161] Bonnie Sher Klein, *Speaking Our Peace*, National Film Board, 1985.

[162] City of Ottawa Archives, Marion Dewar Fonds, Box A2010-0765, folder 5. See "thank-you" for her visit September 30, 1982, from Barbara MacKinnon, then the director. "Mayor Dewar was a public health nurse for several years, and learned a great deal about mental health problems in the Ottawa Area." Causeway Newsletter, included with the letter.

[163] City of Ottawa Archives, Marion Dewar Fonds, Box A2010-0765, folder 4, correspondence & clippings, April 1981.

[164] City of Ottawa Archives, Marion Dewar Fonds, Box A2010-0765, folder 9, correspondence with Sharon Rusu.

[165] City of Ottawa Archives, Marion Dewar Fonds, Box A2010-0765 folder 5, Marion Dewar to Holly McKay of the Centre: 11/16/1982: "Comments about Feminists causing certain victories was a welcome sound." For the Bookstore, to which she lent $1,000 when they were strapped for funds, see City of Ottawa Archives, Marion Dewar Fonds, A2010-0765, File 5 Mayor's Personal Correspondence, 1982, folder 5.

[166] This is the title of Penney Kome's account: *The Taking of Twenty-Eight: Women Challenge the Constitution* (Toronto: Women's Educational Press, 1983). Thanks to Constance Backhouse, who suggested this reference.

[167] City of Ottawa Archives, Marion Dewar Fonds, A2010-0767. "Interview by Debra Pilon," *Herizons*, December 1985.

[168] See Kome. Axworthy referred to the Ad Hoc Conference women as "'Cadillac feminists'" But not all agree. Some think he's received a raw deal: articles taking this point of view will appear in a forthcoming issue of *Atlantis*.

[169] For Anderson's account of her resignation, see Doris Anderson, *Rebel Daughter: An Autobiography* (Toronto: Key Porter Books, 1996), 246, 238–9.

[170] From *Herizons* interview, op cit. Kome acknowledges Dewar's role; Anderson does not.

[171] On Jewett and Section 28, see Judith McKenzie, *Pauline Jewett,* 124–125. On Mitchell, see Margaret Mitchell, *No Laughing Matter: Adventure, Activism & Politics* (Granville Island, BC: Granville Island Publishing, 2008), 158 and ff.

[172] E.C. LeSage, "Policy-Making at City Hall: Ottawa's Office of Equal Opportunity for Women," in *Urban Politics in Ottawa-Carleton, Research Essays*, Second Edition, Donald G. Rowat, ed. (Ottawa: Department of Political Science, Carleton University, 1983), 186.

[173] City of Ottawa Archives, Marion Dewar Fonds, A2006-0116, box 30 contains a bound volume of equal opportunity for women advisory committee minutes, April 1980 to November 1980. Kehoe quotation is from July 18, 1980 in camera meeting.

[174] Maude Barlow, *The Fight of My Life: Confessions of an Unrepentant Canadian* (Toronto: HarperCollins, 1998). For her appointment, see 42.

[175] See Patricia Kearns's 1998 NFB film *Democracy a la Maude*, for a wonderful view of Barlow. http://nfb.ca/film/democracy_a_la_maude/, accessed June 4, 2016.

[176] Constance Backhouse, "Sexual Harassment: A Feminist Phrase that Transformed the Workplace," *Canadian Journal of Women and the Law*, vol 24, no. 2 (2012): 275–300. See also Constance Backhouse and Leah Cohen, *The Secret Oppression: Sexual Harassment of Working Women* (Toronto: Macmillan, 1978), in which the authors point out that sexual harassment, like rape, is an "expression of power," 38–52.

[177] City of Ottawa Archives, Marion Dewar Fonds, A2010-0765, File 5.

"Mayor's Personal Correspondence," 1982, Barlow's letter dated 1/8/1982.

[178] Amen Jafri, "The Town that Fun Forgot?" https://www.youtube.com/watch?v=CKk_kRSTaOc, accessed June 4, 2016.

[179] City of Ottawa Archives, Marion Dewar Fonds, A2010-0406 #89, file number 3.

[180] Ibid.

[181] See City of Ottawa Archives, Marion Dewar Fonds, A2010-0765 folder 1, Susan Geraldine Taylor's bill to "Her Worship" October 27, 1983.

[182] Gunda Lambton, *Stealing the Show: Seven Women Artists in Canadian Public Art* (Montreal and Kingston: McGill-Queen's University Press, 1994), 107 ff.

[183] City of Ottawa Archives, Marion Dewar Fonds, A2010-0765, Card from Baslaw to the mayor 12/17/1984, folder 8, 1984.

[184] City of Ottawa Archives, Marion Dewar Fonds, A2010-0406 # 89, for the Mayor's Advisory Group on Arts and Culture.

[185] City of Ottawa Archives, Marion Dewar Fonds, A2010-0406 Box 89 folder, 8. "Proposals for Development of Arts and Culture in the Ottawa-Carleton Region: A Report for Mayor Marion Dewar prepared on behalf of the Mayor's Advisory Group on Arts and Culture" by Tom Henighan, Sept. 1980.

[186] City of Ottawa Archives, Marion Dewar Fonds, 2010 0406 #89, "Region Subsidizing Ottawa," *Ottawa Citizen*, October 28, 1980, 5.

[187] City of Ottawa Archives, Marion Dewar Fonds, Box A2010-1416, Box 89, Information about and minutes of the meeting at Glebe Community Centre, 10/29/1980.

[188] City of Ottawa Archives, Marion Dewar Fonds, A2010-0407, Box #90 folder 11, Rideau Centre. Letter to Marion Dewar, then a controller, from Ken Hawkins, dated May Day 1978. Marion Dewar to Ken Hawkins, letter dated June 9, 1978.

[189] City of Ottawa Archives, Marion Dewar Fonds, A2010-0407 Box 90 file 11, Rideau Centre, letter.

[190] *Ottawa Journal*, June 24, 1980: http://newspapers.com/newspage/41547893/, accessed June 4, 2016.

[191] Thomas Piketty, *Capital in the Twenty-First Century*. Arthur Goldhammer, trans. (Cambridge, MA: Harvard University Press, 2014), 42: "The growth of capital's share accelerated with the victories of Margaret Thatcher in England in 1979 and Ronald Reagan in the United States in 1980, marking the beginning of a conservative revolution."

"Audrey McLaughlin just might do
it." Marion and others, working with
McLaughlin on her successful campaign
to become leader of the New Democratic
Party in 1989. McLaughlin is to the left,
and Dewar is to the right.

Chapter 5
FEDERAL POLITICS

Marion Dewar decided not to run for mayor of Ottawa in 1985, although many people thought she should. Toddy Kehoe told me that Dewar was so popular she could have run successfully, not only in 1985, but also for several terms thereafter.

In public, Dewar stated that she had decided not to run again because both she and the city needed a change: "I needed new challenges and the mayor's chair needed a new face."[192] More privately, she may well have been discouraged by the 1982 results. Although she had beaten her opponent Darrel Kent handily, her campaign team noted that Kent had done relatively well in the outlying suburban sections of the city. Dewar and others saw this – correctly – as a harbinger of change. The city would continue to expand, and voters in the outlying regions would be less sympathetic to progressive ideas than those who lived in Ottawa's downtown neighbourhoods.[193] Dewar had made her decision to step down by July 1985, when she ran for and was acclaimed president of the New Democratic Party.

From the time she left office as mayor until 1993, she was involved in federal politics as a New Democrat. She already had experience at the provincial and federal levels. She ran at the provincial level in 1977, lost, and was, according to her daughter Liz, deeply disappointed. In 1984, she could have run in the federal riding of Ottawa Centre. (This is the riding, much expanded today, for which her son Paul Dewar was Member of Parliament from 2006 to 2015.) She was encouraged to do so by influential Ottawa New

Democrats, but she declined.[194] Michael Cassidy had decided to run, and instead of challenging his bid for the nomination, she worked hard on his campaign.

Michael Cassidy won the riding in 1984 by a scant 59 votes. When I interviewed him in 2012, Cassidy told me that Dewar did not simply back away from contesting the nomination, she went door-to-door canvassing for him. Marion Dewar genuinely enjoyed talking to voters at their front doors and, in turn, voters responded to her with enthusiasm. "She stepped in and supported me," Cassidy told me. "She took on the Glebe [a downtown neighbourhood] while she was mayor…she got me elected…I am eternally grateful."[195]

PRESIDENT OF THE NDP

Dewar's first venture in her own right into federal politics – her two years as president of the New Democratic Party – did not turn out well. The presidency of the NDP has some peculiar features. The position was, and still is, unpaid, but it is an important one. The president is the administrative chair of the NDP, and an administrator can have a considerable amount of power. But for Dewar, "[it] was one of the toughest and unhappiest two years I spent in a working environment…."[196] When asked if it would "have been easier if you had been a man?", Dewar replied that, yes, indeed it would have been. "I wasn't one of the boys." Evelyn Gigantes remarked to me that "subsequently, both NDP women leaders went through special difficulties because they were women." She adds, "I'm sure that Marion ran into the same kind of struggles, as she pre-dated them in her position as president within the Party."

Dewar did have an agenda as NDP president. Her goal was to broaden the party's scope, "to build the party." She wanted more presence and more power for women in the NDP, and less power for "party bureaucrats and politicians." She came to the presidency with the aim of having "fifty per cent women" as NDP candidates. We can surmise that the party bureaucrats and politicians definitely did not take kindly to this idea. The New Democrats did nominate more women candidates than the other major parties (40 per cent), but not often in "winnable" ridings.[197]

When she became president in July 1985, she was acclaimed, even though, by her own account a decade later, a lot of members of the party had opposed her. Michael Cassidy moved her nomination: "And Mike Cassidy gave a wonderful speech, he nominated me and said, 'this was the toughest, it was the most contested acclamation he had ever been around.'"[198]

Dewar wrestled with the president's job for two years, resigning in 1987 to run in a by-election for the federal riding of Hamilton-Mountain. The seat became vacant when Ian Deans, the NDP incumbent, resigned to become chairman of the Public Services Relations Board. The New Democrats took all three ridings in the by-elections held on July 20, 1987. One of the other winners was Audrey McLaughlin, elected for the Yukon, whom Marion Dewar would later back as leader of the NDP, and with whom she would develop a close friendship and working relationship.

MP FOR HAMILTON-MOUNTAIN

How did Dewar come to be nominated by the Hamilton-Mountain riding association? Was she a "parachute" candidate? Brian Charlton – who was an Ontario MPP and a cabinet minister in Bob Rae's government, and who told me he has been "active in every [NDP] campaign on the Mountain since 1963" – says, "Some saw Marion as a parachute candidate, most did not. My father, John Charlton, my mother, Jean Charlton, a significant number of party activists in the Riding and from across the City…formed an impressive group who convinced Marion to seek the nomination."

Dewar would be MP for Hamilton-Mountain for eighteen months. She was a dedicated, hardworking Member of Parliament. Charlton, who knew her well – they shared a constituency office – says she was good "in the riding and in the House." She had been appointed NDP critic for the status of women, employment, and community economic development. Given that fact, it is not surprising that such issues took up much of her time. She gave her vigorous support to the postal workers during a strike in progress in the summer of 1987, when she had just become MP. She faulted the Progressive Conservative government and Prime Minister Mulroney himself for not intervening and stated repeatedly that Canada Post's proposal to institute a two-tier wage system in the postal service would have a particularly unfortunate effect on "the handicapped, ethnic minorities, and women."[199] In Hamilton, she took up the cause of women who had been sexually harassed at the Dofasco plant.[200]

And on the issue of abortion, after the Supreme Court of Canada had struck down Canada's existing abortion legislation, overturning an Ontario appeal court ruling against abortion activist Dr. Henry Morgentaler, she recalled a decade later: "We had a wonderful debate in the House on the whole choice issue." During this debate, which took place during January and February 1988, MP Dewar worked with other women MPs across party lines, including Progressive Conservatives Barbara McDougall and Flora MacDonald. Dewar remembers that MacDonald commented to her: "Marion, you know, if we don't do this, there's enough people in the House that we could have abortions totally illegal again...."[201]

Dewar spoke in the debate: "It is essential, Mr. Speaker, that the Tory government clearly indicate to Canadian women, physicians, and provincial governments that Section 252 of the Criminal Code can no longer set the procedure through which therapeutic abortion services are made available." Then she went on to talk about "the real challenge underlying the entire matter. A broad range of health services should be made available to Canadian women. For that purpose, the federal government should finance the search for safe and effective contraceptive methods as well as the education programs of responsible organizations such as the Planned Parenthood Federation."[202] Although Dewar, understandably, remembered the work women Members of Parliament did across party lines, male as well as female Members of the House of Commons supported new legislation guaranteeing a woman's right to choose abortion. (If men had not supported the measure, it never would have passed the House.) NDP leader Ed Broadbent spoke eloquently in support of changes to the law on January 29, 1988.[203]

The House of Commons approved new legislation, but the Senate did not. The consequent impasse meant that no legislation was passed. But the Criminal Code provisions struck down by the Supreme Court of Canada no longer operated. We are still waiting for "the broad range of health services" for which Dewar advocated.

When it came to re-election, Dewar was not successful. She was defeated in the November 21, 1988, federal election by a heartbreaking seventy-nine votes, losing to the Liberal candidate, Beth Phinny.

Brian Charlton says that Dewar lost this election because she made "very serious mistakes...dozens of canvassers, including myself, told her she was running the wrong campaign with the wrong focus and the wrong targets, but she didn't listen." Dewar would attribute her defeat to the fact that New Democrats in the riding had become complacent. "Mostly they thought it was our riding." She had specific criticisms for the steelworkers in Hamilton-Mountain. "They are," she said, "a great part of Hamilton." (They were then. This is no longer the case.) She believed they did not come out in sufficient numbers to campaign for her. But Brian Charlton asserts that Dewar exaggerated their importance to the NDP in 1988. "I think the legend of the steelworkers as a political force in Hamilton was bigger in Marion's mind than in reality."

Ed Broadbent and David MacKenzie, who in 1988 had worked with the United Steelworkers in Hamilton for many years, both say, as Charlton does, that Dewar was wrong about the steelworkers. "I'd be amazed if that were the case," said Broadbent. "Steelworkers were and are very good on women." David MacKenzie commented as follows: "To your queries about the steelworkers: it's difficult to imagine that any sort of 'lukewarm' sentiment about Marion's feminism played a part in her defeat in 1988. Starting in the late 70s, the union had begun taking women's equality issues very seriously, had dubbed their emerging women's committees as 'Women of Steel,' and in the late 80s had launched a particular (and very complicated) effort to refashion the union's job evaluation program (called Cooperative Wage Study at the time) in order to eliminate accrued gender biases in its application." Brian Charlton agrees: "The steelworkers have done magnificent work on women's issues."

Ed Broadbent, David MacKenzie, and Brian Charlton are all commenting in good faith, and they are most likely correct. But a feminist can nonetheless question their capacity to fully grasp the nature of discrimination against women in a male-dominated industry such as steel manufacturing. For example, there remains that difficult question about sexual harassment at Dofasco in the 1980s, although as Brian Charlton points out, the Dofasco workers were not part of the steelworkers. Charlton says, "If the steelworkers had been the bargaining agent in Dofasco, they would have taken on the issue as they did in Stelco and dozens of other plants."

AUDREY MCLAUGHLIN AND THE NDP LEADERSHIP

Following her defeat in the general election of 1988, Dewar continued to be active in the New Democratic Party. She was most notably one of the group of women who campaigned for the successful nomination of Audrey McLaughlin as the leader of the federal NDP. Dewar herself says, "I was very active in her campaign."[204] McLaughlin confirms this. In her memoir, *A Woman's Place: My Life and Politics*, she says that Dewar launched her campaign and went on to make sure it succeeded.

Ed Broadbent resigned on March 4, 1989. The campaign to replace him began immediately. There were several men in the race, including Dave Barrett, who had been premier of British Columbia, and Bob Rae, the provincial leader of the New Democrats in Ontario. According to Audrey McLaughlin, Dewar could have been a candidate: "Marion Dewar, although she had lost her seat in the election, seemed another strong potential candidate."[205] But, says McLaughlin:

> Marion…had another individual in mind. Hugh Winsor, Ottawa correspondent for *The Globe and Mail*, approached her after Ed's speech and asked whether she thought a woman would run. Her reply? "Audrey McLaughlin just might do it." Marion had not yet mentioned this idea to me, so I was somewhat surprised when Hugh asked if I was running. I told him, quite honestly, that I hadn't even considered it. "Well, your press agent is already at work," he reported.[206]

There were a number of possible women candidates, according to McLaughlin, but none of them wanted to take on the task. "Both Pauline Jewett and Marion Dewar wanted me to run. Marion, a very tenacious woman, kicked her machine into gear."[207]

The NDP leadership convention was held in Winnipeg, and on December 2, 1989, McLaughlin became the leader after a hotly contested race that went to four ballots. Her main opponent was Dave Barrett. Taking over from Broadbent, McLaughlin was the first woman in Canada's history to lead a party with MPs in the House of Commons.

Audrey McLaughlin took over the party leadership when the NDP was a force to be reckoned with. The years of her leadership were tumultuous, seeing, for example, the rise of the Reform Party in western Canada and the separatist Bloc Québécois in Quebec.

The October 25, 1993, federal election was a rout for the New Democrats, as it was, of course, for the Progressive Conservatives. The New Democrats elected so few members that the party lost its official party status. Was this Audrey McLaughlin's fault? It most likely was not, although it was easy to blame her, and Jill Vickers, a political scientist and an experienced New Democrat, told me, "The women made mistakes. Audrey McLaughlin really wasn't ready to be leader. She didn't have the experience." Marion Dewar ran in the election of 1993, in the riding of Ottawa Centre. She lost, and lost definitively. She was deeply disappointed, and the failed bid did mark the end of her sojourn in federal politics. She asserted later that she was asked to make a bid for the leadership of the NDP after 1993, but her reply was that she did not have a seat in the House, and therefore could not run for leader.[208]

"IF I DO NOT HAVE TO GO TO QUESTION PERIOD, I CAN SURVIVE TODAY."

The most remarkable fact about Marion Dewar's foray into federal politics is that she did not enjoy it. She certainly did not like being party president, as we have seen. But she did not always like being a Member of Parliament either. Being an MP for Hamilton-Mountain was hard on her personal life. Her children were grown and Ken supported her, but she did not enjoy spending time away from her home, from St. Basil's Church, and from her involvement with Ottawa concerns and Ottawa friends. She was lonely in Hamilton, and when the House was sitting and she was in Ottawa, she was working all the time.

Moreover, there were aspects of the milieu of the House of Commons that she found not merely difficult, but alienating. Dewar truly hated question period. As she told Greta Hofmann Nemiroff, question period was confrontational and it encouraged the worst sort of male posturing. When Hofmann Nemiroff asked her, "Did you feel respected?" Dewar answered, "More so as mayor than I did in the House. The House is a very demeaning.... Oh it's dreadful! It's horrible!" She would say to herself, "If I don't have to go to question period, I can survive today." Dewar did not like the NDP caucus either: "I also found caucus very unstimulating. I thought our caucuses were so awful."[209]

Although Dewar did have negative feelings about question period and about debate in the House, she handled that aspect of a Member of Parliament's duties with courage and assurance. She rose often in the House not only in question period but in debate, speaking, for example, about refugees and the government's proposed amendment to the Immigration Act of 1976 about refugee determination:

> Mr. Speaker...people want to have a fair Immigration Act...the [government's] Bill is not a fair Bill. It is a Bill that will discriminate against refugee designation...I believe all Canadians are proud of our country, which has been built from the different ethnic backgrounds of people who have come here in various ways.... I believe we have also been careful to ensure that people remain in contact with their own cultures so that they do not deny their roots. This has enriched the fabric of Canada....

She also spoke out vigorously in support of affordable housing for women:

> The Minister has expressed her concern about the lack of affordable housing for women....Therefore will she be proposing a specific program to her cabinet colleagues in order to relieve these women of the suffering they are enduring?... Private developers are not building affordable housing...and the government is not increasing its quota.... Would the Minister please tell the House whether she is willing to work with the Minister responsible for CMHC to see there are more units on the market?

In December 1987, she spoke in question period about the dangers of pornography. It was not so much pornography itself that troubled her, but rather the real violence against women and children of which it was a symptom:

> Mr. Speaker...as a feminist I abhor the type of pornography available to our children, our young people, and adults in society... we [need] to bring forward legislation, which indicates that we will not accept the fact that children and women can be looked at in a demeaning way.... For a pornography Bill to be a positive one, it must look at what happens in society and how we feel about violence....[210]

These are just three examples taken from scores of other occasions when Dewar spoke in the House of Commons during her sixteen months as an M P.[211]

In *A Woman's Place*, Audrey McLaughlin discusses her own alienation from federal politics and her bond with Marion Dewar. McLaughlin and Dewar were both elected to the House of Commons for the first time in the summer of 1987. It appears that a bond arose between them almost at once, and with good reason. Each had trained in and practised a women's helping profession – Dewar as a nurse and McLaughlin as a social worker. Both were deeply concerned with social justice and with the cause of peace.

From McLaughlin's point of view, the House of Commons was a "men's club."

She, like Dewar, was disheartened by question period: "I remember how amazed Marion and I were when we sat through our first question period. The posturing, the banging on desks, and the shouting made us think of school kids."[212] During Audrey McLaughlin's leadership, Marion Dewar continued to give her friend and colleague her support and counsel:

> Of all the people helping keep my feet on the ground and my courage up in those exciting but difficult early days, Marion Dewar proved especially invaluable. Without her urging, I likely would never have run for the leadership in the first place. Now that I'd won, she undoubtedly felt some responsibility to make sure that I survived, but it went far beyond that. If I had a cold, Marion would show up on the doorstep with fresh orange juice. If I had a problem with the caucus, Marion had a solution. If I despaired of ever becoming truly fluent in French, Marion would repeat her favourite line, "You'll learn." She is without question one of the most sensitive, compassionate, and nurturing people I know.[213]

Dewar ran in three federal elections and lost twice. Her time as a Member of Parliament was relatively brief. In contrast, Audrey McLaughlin was not only the NDP's first woman leader, she sat as Member of Parliament for the Yukon from 1987 to 1997, after running successfully in 1988 and 1993. McLaughlin may have experienced the House of Commons as a men's club, but she learned to adapt. It is my guess that Dewar would have done so, had she been able to retain her seat in Hamilton-Mountain. Indeed, she might have been able to bring some measure of consensus and conciliation to the caucus and to question period.

During Dewar's years as party president and as Member of Parliament, Ed Broadbent was the party's leader. If federal politics was a men's club, Ed Broadbent was part of that club. To the extent that the New Democratic Party was male-dominated, Broadbent, whatever his own views actually were or are on women and men, was the chief representative of that domination.

In November 2013, when Ed Broadbent sat down with me to discuss Marion Dewar, he had only praise for her, although he emphasized her strength and passion rather than her commitment to consensus: "She was – like Pauline Jewett – an independent spirit...the flip side of strong personalities – this is not in any way critical – she was strong.... She was not always easy. Such strong people are not." [She was] "determined to get things done. Yes, she could be collaborative, and she certainly was a team player. But her perspective was: 'Let's get this done.' If you had to be collaborative to get it done, she could do that."

There is some evidence that there were tensions between Marion Dewar and Ed Broadbent when she was party president, and when she was Member of Parliament. She said so herself to Hofmann Nemiroff. If we contemplate the meanings of power and gender in Canada in the 1980s (and today), these tensions should come as no surprise. Federal politicians in Canada wield power. If a woman displays an interest in power or authority, then and now, many people believe that she has transgressed gender roles.

Former Liberal politician Sheila Copps once said, "If you're a woman and you're aggressive, you're a ball-buster."[214] Copps was a politician, not a theorist, but in fact feminist theorists have discussed at length the difficulties women face if they seek power today or sought it in the past.[215] For example, literary critic Carolyn Heilbrun has written on women, anger, and power. About anger, she says (making the same point as Copps): "To denounce women for shrillness and stridency is another way of denying them any right to power." Women, says Heilbrun, are taught to suppress anger and to avoid power. "Although feminists early discovered that the private is the public, women's exercise of power and control, and the admission and expression of anger necessary to that exercise, has until recently been declared unacceptable."[216]

Women struggle – and often lose – in specific male-dominated environments. The environment Dewar had to contend with from 1985 to 1993 was that of Canadian federal politics. In 1921, Agnes Macphail was the first woman elected to Canada's House of Commons. Macphail thought she would soon be joined by numerous other women: "I could almost hear them coming," she is reported to have said.[217]

But Macphail was wrong. She was the sole woman for more than a decade. When Dewar entered Parliament in 1987, women made up less than 10 per cent of the House of Commons. The numbers have improved since then, but women still made up less than 25 per cent before the federal election of October 19, 2015. After the election the figure rose to 26 per cent.

The House of Commons was male-dominated in terms of numbers, as it still is, but also in terms of attitudes. In the spring of 1982, when NDP MP Margaret Mitchell rose to speak about wife beating, Members of the House of Commons greeted her remarks with derisive laughter.[218] Such egregious misogyny would not occur in today's House of Commons, even though women's issues still receive short shrift.

Mitchell, like Dewar, experienced the House of Commons as oppressively male:

When I arrived in Ottawa in 1979 I was shocked at the male-dominated culture. As I entered the Parliament building, I was usually stopped by security staff, who assumed since I was a woman that I was a secretary. Washrooms for women were not as available as those for men. The language of documents and parliamentary reports was always masculine. (I strongly opposed this when I was briefly on the Members' Committee in 1987; I was not reappointed.) A general air of male superiority dominated the halls of power.[219]

In later life, Marion Dewar very much enjoyed her grandchildren and great-grandchildren. Here she is with Bob's baby daughter, Maeghan. 1983.

Dewar left federal politics in 1993 for a number of reasons. First of all, she lost in Ottawa Centre and she found this defeat hard to take, in part because she lost to Mac Harb, a ferociously adversarial campaigner. Audrey McLaughlin was one of many people who wrote her to bemoan her defeat: "You have such a special quality of supporting women (and men when deserved) and being clear, in a way I am not, about where we should be going politically as a party, as women." The defeat would have been difficult for a seasoned male politician, but such a person would likely have overcome it.[220] After all, no New Democratic candidates won in Ontario in 1993. But Jill Vickers, who told me that Dewar was "not a career politician" was right, I think, and I believe the most important factor influencing Dewar to withdraw from federal politics was her deep dismay concerning the relentless hold that patriarchy continued to have in Canada's corridors of power. Yes, she believed in working from within, as she did with the church for example, or as she did as a local politician. But she could not stomach the machismo that dominated federal politics.

While Dewar wanted more women to enter politics, she never believed that women – simply because they were women – would transform society, although she did believe that numbers mattered. ("Women in power in numbers will achieve peace," she said in the 1987 National Film Board film, *A Love Affair with Politics: A Portrait of Marion Dewar*.) She worked across party lines with women like Red Tory Flora MacDonald, but what she wanted, at all political levels, was the involvement of women and men who supported social justice over selfishness and consensus over competitiveness.

In her book *Toeing the Lines*, Canadian political scientist Sylvia Bashevkin writes about Canadian women's rights advocates of the nineteenth and early twentieth century. For these suffragist activists, says Bashevkin, there were tensions between "independence vs. partisanship." They wanted an alliance of women independent of "partyism": "Major streams within Canadian suffragism rejected the evils of 'partyism' in favour of an independent, virtually suprapolitical posture."[221] The few women MPs from all political parties elected in the 1970s and 1980s also rejected "partyism." The difficulties besetting this position, Bashevkin suggests, were virtually insurmountable in the early period. They remained so in the 1980s and they remain so today. Political parties, caucuses, competitive rivalries, the posturing of debate and of question period are part of the fabric of federal political life. Women who succeed in politics at Canada's federal level or elsewhere around the world tend to be co-opted by the milieu in which they must inevitably work.

In 1993, Marion Dewar was sixty-five years old. She could have retired from public life. However, although she never ran for public office again, she remained a passionate and committed activist right up until her death in September 2008, speaking eloquently at the Ottawa Art Gallery on September 4, 2008, about society's need for the arts: "If we let the arts slip, we'll let our civilization slip."[222]

Dewar's most contentious activity during the 1990s was the work she did as member of the Ottawa-Carleton Police Services Board. The board had been created by the NDP Ontario provincial government, which was elected in 1990. The board's purpose was to oversee the merger of the Ottawa, Nepean, and Gloucester police forces. Ontario premier Bob Rae appointed Marion Dewar and she chaired the board. But when Mike Harris's Conservatives won provincially in 1995, Premier Harris moved quickly to fire Dewar and three other NDP appointees to the board. Dewar and one other fired member successfully sued the government for wrongful dismissal.[223]

In the 1990s, she worked for the Canadian branch of the international charity Oxfam, with which her former executive assistant and friend Robert Fox had long been involved. Dewar was chair of Oxfam Canada's Board of Directors from 1994 to 1999. On her death, Oxfam Canada created a women's leadership fund in honour of their "champion and mentor."[224]

Marion Dewar also volunteered her time to Carleton University, from which both her sons had graduated. She sat on Carleton's Board of Governors from 1990 to 1999, serving as the board's vice-chair from 1997 to 1999.[225]

In the summer of 2003 she gave her assistance to Monia Mazigh's valiant and ultimately successful effort to gain freedom for her husband, Maher Arar. In 2002, Maher Arar was deported to Syria from New York and imprisoned in Syria. The Canadian government (Jean Chrétien was prime minister) appeared to be doing little to press for his release, and it seemed that he might well be imprisoned indefinitely. Dewar worked with Alex Neve of Amnesty

Marion receives a present from younger
family members. This was after 2007
(the publication date of *Shock Doctrine*),
near the end of her life.

International. She appeared at a press conference held on August 7, 2003, with Mazigh and Neve. "Marion spoke to demand, along with Amnesty, that the Canadian government take action."[226]

Marion Dewar received many honours during the last years of her life. Among them was an honorary degree from Carleton University on June 15, 2000.[227] The most significant was the Order of Canada, the country's highest civilian honour, which she was awarded in May of 2002. The investiture took place in February 2003.

During the last years of her life, however, Dewar was overwhelmed by the problems she had to confront in her personal life, the most demanding of which was Ken Dewar's final illness. He suffered from lung disease, and in his last years he needed oxygen and extensive nursing care. According to their daughter Liz, "He went through cancer, remission, but ultimately it was emphysema that got him.... It was a good ten years that he had his lung disease." Dewar not only loved Ken, she was also a nurse. She knew that Ken did not want to go to hospital, and she managed to see that he did not. "She was so stubborn and determined to just tough it out herself...she was determined that he was going to die at home and that she was going to look after him."

Ken Dewar did die at home "peacefully, Tuesday, April 22, 2003, surrounded by his family...."[228] But nursing him wore Marion Dewar out. Not only did she lose weight, she was exhausted. A heart condition she already suffered from worsened. She had heart surgery and thereafter had to take blood thinners.

Her death in September 2008 was an accident exacerbated by the blood thinners. She went to Toronto to enjoy the Toronto International Film Festival. She had the misfortune to trip and fall on the sidewalk, hitting her head. She was taken to hospital, but she never recovered. With her while she could still talk was her niece Gail, who lives in Toronto and was the first family member to reach her. Gail says her Aunt Marion did say, "I'm coming, Ken." Soon after she fell into a coma and died on September 15, 2008. Her funeral was held in Ottawa on September 19. Father Corbin Eddy, who had been parish priest at St. Basil's, celebrated the Mass and gave the homily.[229] Father Eddy began with a poem by the Israeli poet Yehuda Amichai:

The Place Where We Are Right
From the place where we are right
Flowers will never grow
In the spring.

The place where we are right
Is hard and trampled
Like a yard.

But doubts and loves
Dig up the world
Like a mole, a plough.
And a whisper will be heard in the place
Where the ruined
House once stood.

Marion Dewar, said Father Eddy, was a plough: she did "dig up the world" to make it a better place.

ENDNOTES:

[192] City of Ottawa Archives, Marion Dewar Fonds, A 2010 0765, folder 9. Dewar to Michael Church, president of the Ottawa-Carleton Board of Trade, 4/2/1985.

[193] City of Ottawa Archives, A 2010 0767 Box 5 "1982 elections: organization."

[194] City of Ottawa Archives, Marion Dewar Fonds, A2010 0765, folder 8. Clyde Sanger correspondence, July 1984.

[195] City of Ottawa Archives, Marion Dewar Fonds, A2010 0765, folder 8. See Cassidy's letter of thanks to Dewar 9/18/1984.

[196] Hofmann Nemiroff interview.

[197] See Brodie, 21 and ch. 7 for the New Democrats. For the number of MPs, see Sylvia Bashevkin, "Women's Representation in the House of Commons: A Stalemate?" *Canadian Parliamentary Review*, vol. 39, no. 1 (2011): "As reported in Table 1, data on women MPs during the past two decades show the percentage of seats they held increased markedly from the 1984 level of about 10% to the 1997 level of more than 20%." http://www.revparl.ca/34/1/34n1_11e_Bashevkin.pdf, accessed June 4, 2016.

[198] Hofmann Nemiroff interview.

[199] City of Ottawa Archives, Marion Dewar Fonds, A2010 0767, Box 3, "Federal MP Correspondence, 1987."

[200] City of Ottawa Archives, Marion Dewar Fonds, A 2010 0767 Box 3, "Federal MP Correspondence, 1987," letter from Carolyn Balogh.

[201] Hofmann Nemiroff interview. On the question of abortion and Brian Mulroney's cabinet, see "Mulroney-era documents reveal struggle with abortion laws": http://www.cbc.ca/news/politics/mulroney-era-documents-reveal-struggle-with-abortion-laws-1.2430081, accessed June 4, 2016.

[202] House of Commons, Debates, 33rd Parliament, 2nd Session, vol. 10, 2/2/1988, p. 12524.

[203] House of Commons, Debates, 33rd Parliament, 2nd Session, 1/29/1988, p 12426.

[204] Hofmann Nemiroff interview.

[205] Audrey McLaughlin with Rick Archibald, *A Woman's Place: My Life and Politics* (Toronto: Macfarlane Walter & Ross, 1992), 52.

[206] Ibid.

[207] Ibid. 53.

[208] Hofmann Nemiroff interview.

[209] Ibid.

[210] House of Commons Debates, 33rd Parliament, 2nd Session: Vol. 9, 11422, 12/7/1987. For the bill being debated, see L. Casevant and J. Robertson, "The Evolution of Pornography Law in Canada," Parliament of Canada Research Paper (2007), http://parl.gc.ca/Content/LOP/researchpublications/843-e. htm#currentlaw.

[211] For refugees, see House of Commons Debates, 33rd Parliament, 2nd session, 8/18/1987, 8176. The House, prorogued, had been recalled to debate C-55. For affordable housing for women, see House of Commons Debates, 33rd Parliament, Second Session, 9/16/1987, 8996. "Several Honourable Members" cried out "Oh, oh!" when Dewar criticized private developers.

[212] McLaughlin, 27.

[213] McLaughlin, 92–3.

[214] See Jane Arscott and Linda Trimble (December 20, 2002). "Where have all the women leaders gone?" University of Alberta ExpressNews.

[215] The literature on this question is extensive, including Natalie Zemon Davis, *Society and Culture in Early Modern France: Eight Essays* (Stanford, CA: Stanford University Press, 1975) and Joan Kelly, *Women, History, and Theory: The Essays of Joan Kelly* (Chicago: University of Chicago Press, 1984).

[216] Carolyn G. Heilbrun, *Writing a Woman's Life* (New York: W. W. Norton & Company, 1988), 16-17.

[217] See Bashevkin (2011), http://www.revparl.ca/34/1/34n1_11e_Bashevkin. pdf, accessed June 4, 2016.

[218] Mitchell, xii. The date was May 12, 1982.

[219] Mitchell, 149.

[220] City of Ottawa Archives, Marion Dewar Fonds, A20100766, 16, McLaughlin letter.

[221] Sylvia B. Bashevkin, *Toeing the Lines: Women and Party Politics in English Canada* (Toronto: University of Toronto Press, 1985), 8.

[222] For this speech, see Doug Fischer's obituary of Dewar, *Ottawa Citizen* September 15, 2008.

[223] Thomas Claridge (July 29, 1996). "Tory actions illegal, court rules". *The Globe and Mail*. A7.

[224] http://oxfam.ca/donate/marion-dewar-fund-for-womens-leadership, accessed June 4, 2016.

[225] These dates taken from the citation (in my possession) read when Dewar received her Honourary Degree from Carleton in 2000.

[226] Monia Mazigh, *Hope & Despair: My Struggle to Free My Husband, Maher Arar*, Patricia Claxton and Fred A. Reed trans. (Toronto: McClelland & Stewart, 2008), 162–163.

[227] I had the honour of presenting her and reading the citation when I was a professor at Carleton University. There is also the Marion Dewar Prize, established in 2004 in her honour by the National Capital Committee on the Scholarship, Preservation, and Dissemination of Women's History, and the Marion Dewar Scholarship Fund of the Ottawa Community Immigrant Services.

[228] Kenneth Dewar obituary: *Ottawa Citizen*, April 23, 2003.

[229] You can find a description of the homily at http://drdawgsblawg. ca/2008/09/farewell-marion.shtml, accessed June 4, 2016.

CONCLUSION

On January 17, 1991, when the first Gulf War broke out, Liz Dewar recalls that her mother was so sickened by the US bombardment of Iraq that she left the family dinner table abruptly and went out into the cold of an Ottawa winter night to compose herself.

Dewar was a woman of passionate conviction. She cared deeply about peace, about social and economic justice, about women's rights, and, of course, about her religious faith. Her beliefs evolved over the years. She was intelligent, but she was never interested in abstractions. She engaged in action. Action meant, for Dewar, picking the right cause (as mayor, taking in Southeast Asian refugees or confronting nepotism at city hall) and then, through a process of conciliation and persuasion, convincing others of the rightness and necessity of that action. As Evelyn Gigantes said to me, "I literally worshipped Marion. Still do: the finest of the fine."

Dewar functioned successfully as a local politician because she acted on the premise that local politics allowed for persuasion and sensible compromise. Indeed it did, in her case. Dewar appears to have believed in the reassuring notion that local government is a "basis of civic education, an apprenticeship in the democratic education of the mass of the people." [230] Local government may provide an opportunity for civic education if a city has an honest, energetic, and skillful mayor like Dewar. If local government is dominated – as it often is – by corrupt individuals who act in collusion with those in the community who have power and control capital, local government will not offer a lesson in democracy.

If local government is so important, some political theorists ask, why don't voters seem to care about it? One undeniable sign of the frailty of local government is the low turnout of voters in civic elections. Voter turnout is low at all levels of government in Canada, but it is worse at the local level than at the provincial or federal levels. [231] But one reason for low voter turnout at the local level is that "considerable effort" is required on the part of the voter. Ballots in civic elections in Canada do not customarily include political party affiliations. Voters must, therefore, inform themselves about the candidate and the issues rather than simply relying on the party label. Local government is not dead or even dying, such theorists affirm, and low voter turnout should not be taken as signalling its demise.

Dewar was a woman in politics and was always conscious of that fact, proud of it and supportive of other women. When she entered city politics in 1972, there were few elected women at the local level. Over the past several decades, the number of women in city politics in Canada has increased, outpacing the numbers at the provincial and federal levels. By the turn of the twenty-first century, there were more women at the local level than at the provincial or federal levels. Many reasons have been put forward to explain why this is the case. Sylvia Bashevkin's argument that early twentieth-century suffragists shunned partyism may still hold. And on a practical level, it is clearly easier to combine the family responsibilities that women still disproportionally shoulder with local as opposed to provincial or federal politics.

Dewar was not only a woman, she was a feminist who brought her feminism to her work as a politician. As mayor, she shared with political scientist Caroline Andrew a vision of a "feminist city." Andrew, in a passionate and provocative article, asks, "A feminist city. What would it look like?"[232]

In her article, Andrew presents us with an answer. A feminist city would include "a network of services designed to reduce and eliminate violence against women, good public transportation, adequate social housing, sufficient daycare, and imaginative urban planning."[233] Such a city, Andrew points out, would be good not only for women, but also for children, the elderly, and the poor.

And how would we get there? Through "feminist political practice and feminist methods of political organizing," that would include the "use of networks and networking" and "a strategy of parallel activity within civil society."[234]

Marion Dewar, during her years as a local politician, did try to build a feminist city, with some success. The gains she made were achieved because she could negotiate and network and she could listen respectfully. Maude Barlow's tenure at the city's Office of Equal Opportunity provides an excellent example in this regard. Barlow would almost certainly not have been appointed at all if Dewar had not been mayor. But beyond that, it was Dewar's steadfast support for Barlow's feminist goals and her ability to persuade or at least sway those who were doubtful (such as policemen and firemen) that made some change possible.

Caroline Andrew has pointed out that local politicians are more likely to experience "intimacy" with their constituents than those elected at the provincial or federal levels. Dewar genuinely enjoyed encounters with members of the community who recognized her, as they frequently did. Her daughter Liz remarked that in the 1970s and 1980s if they went out in public together, Mayor Dewar would be wearing what Liz wryly called her "Carlingwood [shopping centre] smile," and they would stop frequently to allow her mother to shake hands and chat with people. Marion did not tire, but Liz did.

In the Introduction, I promised to explore the connections between Dewar's personal life and her public, political life. I noted that she combined wifehood and motherhood with a public career, and I asked how she negotiated the complex problems these multiple roles presented. The answer, I suggest, is that this was an ongoing struggle. She never did free herself from guilt over the conflicts between her private and her public life.

Some of the feminist theory that analyzes the ways in which the "personal is political" might have been helpful to her. There is the classic work on this subject, Kate Millett's *Sexual Politics*. In it, Millett states boldly that "our society like all other historical civilizations is a patriarchy." The term "politics," says Millett, "shall refer to power-structured relationships, arrangements whereby one group of persons is controlled by another.... A disinterested examination of our system of sexual relationship must point out that the situation between the sexes now, and throughout history, is a…relationship of dominance and subordinance."[235] But there is no evidence that Dewar read Millett.

And then there is the early second-wave feminist analysis of housework. The "Wages for Housework" movement made the cogent point that housework is work, and that societies have always depended on the unpaid labour of women in the family. The coming of capitalism exacerbated this problem. "Work is still work, whether inside or outside the home. The independence of the wage earner means only being a 'free individual' for capital, no less for women than for men…."[236] The flamboyant Marxism of the "Wages for Housework" movement would not have appealed to Dewar, but she would have liked the message that the work women do as housekeepers and as wives and mothers *is work* and deserves to be recognized as such.

I am also guessing that Dewar never read Pat Mainardi's wonderful piece "The Politics of Housework," first published in 1969. It is a riff on the theme that Mainardi's male partner will not share the housework. He likes "liberated women" not "women's liberation," and he will find a way to wriggle out of household chores: "We women," says Mainardi, "have been brainwashed more than even we can imagine. Probably too many years of seeing television women in ecstasy over their shiny-waxed floors or breaking down over their dirty shirt collars. Men have no such conditioning. They recognize the essential fact of housework right from the very beginning. Which is that it stinks."

Marion's husband Ken was extremely supportive of her, but as Mainardi says, "I know that all women have a sore called 'Guilt over a messy house' or 'Household work is ultimately my responsibility.'"[237] Marion Dewar did indeed suffer from that sore, and she never succeeded in overcoming it.

Finally, what should we make of her deep and abiding religious faith? Her faith did not make her the good person she was, nor did her faith make her the skilled, hardworking, and successful local politician she was. Religious faith is more common than goodness, and it is more common than skill and energy. But her commitment to Catholicism was clearly an essential part of the way she lived her life.

There were aspects of her faith that remained traditionally

Catholic. Havi Echenberg, the mayor's staff member, accompanied Dewar to Managua, Nicaragua, in 1983. Dewar was there for a mayors' conference, but in Managua she met with Violetta Chamorro, the widow of Pedro Joaquin Chamorro, who was assassinated by pro-Samoza gunmen in 1978. Violetta Chamorro and Marion Dewar were, as Echenberg put it, "two Catholic women of a certain age." When they met in Chamorro's house, which, Echenberg says, was preserved as a "shrine" to Pedro Joaquin, Dewar asked Chamorro if she had "managed to forgive his murderers." Chamorro's reply was that she had, "because it is the Christian thing to do." After this, says Echenberg, the two women embraced.

We can assume that Dewar believed all her life in the Christian nature of forgiveness. But her evolution from the traditional faith of her girlhood to the radicalism of her maturity – to her advocacy of the ordination of women and support for birth control and a woman's right to choose to have an abortion – is the area of her life in which her remarkable capacity for growth and change most clearly manifested itself.

Marion Dewar was that rare person: a woman who brought to public life her commitment to doing and being good, a woman who worked to benefit the women, men, and children she served. Her life story leaves us with a question: How can more people like her be persuaded to go into public life?

ENDNOTES:

[230] Georges Langrod, "Local Government and Democracy," in *Politics and Government of Urban Canada: Selected Readings*, Second Edition, Lionel D. Feldman and Michael D. Goldrick, eds. (Toronto: Methuen, 1972), 334–335. Langrod argues against the idea that local government inevitably provides lessons in democracy, 4 and passim.

[231] See Graham et al., 93 and ff, on lower voter turn-out. And it got worse, not better, in Ottawa in the 1960s. See Owen Thomas, "Voter Turnout at the Municipal Level," in *Urban Politics in Ottawa-Carleton*, Rowat, ed., 69. In 1960, it was 63.9% overall, but in 1972 had dropped to 32.22%. For the party label, see Graham et al., 96. For provincial and federal levels, see Graham et al., 101.

[232] Caroline Andrew, "The Feminist City," in *Political Arrangements: Power and the City,* Henri Lustiger-Thaler, ed. (Montreal: Black Rose Books, 1992), 109. See also Brodie, passim, and Vickers, et al., 23, ff, and passim.

[233] Andrew (1992), 111.

[234] Ibid., 111–112.

[235] Millett, 23, 24, and 25.

[236] Maria Dalla Costa and Selma James, *The Power of Women and the Subversion of the Community* (Bristol, England: Falling Wall Press, 1972), 11.

[237] See Mainardi's witty piece, first published in 1969: http://www.cwluherstory.org/the-politics-of-housework.html, accessed June 4, 2016.

APPENDIX

LIST OF INTERVIEWEES
Most of the interviews took place in Ottawa. If they took place else-where, or over the telephone, I mention that. Below are the dates of the initial interviews. In some cases there were subsequent inter-views, phone calls, or emails. In all cases, each interviewee approved a transcript of the interview, and in most cases approved the use of their words in the final text. I conducted all of the interviews.

Maude Barlow, by telephone, October 7, 2011
The late Ted Bell (brother of Marion Bell Dewar),
by telephone, February 8, 2012
Florence Stoodley Berndt, February 20, 2012
Sister Aurora Boileau, Kingston, ON, April 10, 2012
Brian Bourns, April 12, 2013
The Honourable Ed Broadbent, November 8, 2013
Michael Cassidy, February 15, 2012
Brian Charlton, by email, January 28, 2015
Bernadette Teresa Burke Cotman, Kingston, ON, April 11, 2012
Robert (Bob) Dewar, by telephone, August 2, 2011,
and subsequent emails and meetings
Cathy Dewar, July 23, 2012
Elizabeth (Liz) Dewar, Kingston, ON, April 10, 2012
Paul Dewar, August 21, 2012
Havi Echenberg, March 12, 2012

Father Corbin Eddy, by telephone, January 9, 2013
Elizabeth Elton, July 18, 2012
Robert Fox, January 30, 2012
Gail Frith (daughter of Marion Bell Dewar's sister, Olive Bell),
by telephone May 29, 2012
The late Sister Loretta Gaffney, April 10, 2012
Barbara and Dan Gamble, July 16, 2012
Evelyn Gigantes, by telephone and email, January 19, 2015
Phillip Goldring, November 21, 2012
Jerry Grey and Susan Geraldine Taylor, November 14, 2011
Tom Henighan, January 25, 2012
Donna Holtom, July 11, 2012
Toddy Kehoe, Chelsea, QC, July 9, 2013
Bruce Laforce, by telephone, October 3, 2011
Can Le, May 23, 2012
Elizabeth Janet Morrissey Lowden, May 15, 2012
Dr Marie Loyer (da Silva), December 10, 2012
The late Honourable Flora MacDonald, August 15, 2012
Russell Mills, October 12, 2012
Elaine Morris, by telephone, August 9, 2012
Dorothy O'Connell, August 9, 2013
Barry Padolsky, December 17, 2013
Sue and George Pike, May 8, 2012
The late Norah Cassidy Renwick, Buckingham, QC,
February 4, 2012
Eleanor Ryan, July 20, 2012
Allan Todd, Buckingham, QC, February 22, 2012
Jill McCalla Vickers, Portland, ON, July 7, 2012
Joan White, February 13, 2013
George Wright, by telephone, February 1, 2012
Lynne Young, August 14, 2012

REFERENCES

MANUSCRIPT COLLECTIONS
City of Ottawa Archives
Religious Hospitallers of St. Joseph-Hotel Dieu (Kingston, Ontario) Archives

NEWSPAPERS
Ottawa Citizen
Ottawa Journal

GOVERNMENT DOCUMENTS
Canadian House of Commons Debates (Hansard)

BOOKS, ARTICLES, UNPUBLISHED MANUSCRIPTS, FILMS, AND AUDIO RECORDINGS
Adamson, Nancy, Linda Briskin, and Margaret McPhail. *Feminist Organizing for Change: The Contemporary Women's Movement in Canada*. Toronto: Oxford University Press, 1988.

Adelman, Howard. *Canada and the Indochinese Refugees*. Regina: L.A. Weigl Educational Associates Ltd., 1982.

Anderson, Doris. *Rebel Daughter: An Autobiography*. Toronto: Key Porter Books, 1996.

Andrew, Caroline. "Ottawa-Hull" in Warren Magnusson and Andrew Sancton, eds. *City Politics in Canada*, 140–165. Toronto: University of Toronto Press, 1983.

——. "The Feminist City," in Henri Lustiger-Thaler, ed. *Political Arrangements: Power and the City*. 109–122. Montreal: Black Rose Books, 1992.

Babcock, Marguerite and Christine McKay, eds. *Challenging Codependency: Feminist Critiques*. Toronto: University of Toronto Press, 1995.

Backhouse, Constance and Leah Cohen. *The Secret Oppression: Sexual Harassment of Working Women*. Toronto: Macmillan, 1978.

Backhouse, Constance. "Sexual Harassment: A Feminist Phrase That Transformed the Workplace." *Canadian Journal of Women and the Law*, vol 24, no. 2, 2012: 275– 300.

Barlow, Maude. *The Fight of My Life: Confessions of an Unrepentant Canadian*. Toronto: HarperCollins, 1998.

Bashevkin, Sylvia B. *Toeing the Lines: Women and Party Politics in English Canada*. Toronto: University of Toronto Press, 1985.

——. "Women's Representation in the House of Commons: A Stalemate?" *Canadian Parliamentary Review*, vol. 39, no. 1, (2011).

Bates, Christina. *A Cultural History of the Nurse's Uniform*. Gatineau, QC: Canadian Museum of Civilization, 2012.

Beiser, Morton. *Strangers at the Gate: The "Boat People's" First Ten Years in Canada*. Toronto: University of Toronto Press, 1999.

Boutilier, Beverly. "Gender, Organized Women, and the Politics of Institution Building: Founding of the Victorian Order of Nurses for Canada, 1893–1900." Ph.D. diss. Carleton University, Ottawa, 1993.

———. "Helpers or Heroines? The National Council of Women, Nursing, and 'Woman's Work' in Late Victorian Canada" in Dianne Dodd and Deborah Gorham, eds. *Caring and Curing: Historical Perspectives on Women and Healing in Canada*. 17–48. Ottawa: University of Ottawa Press, 1994.

Brodie, Janine. *Women and Politics in Canada*. Toronto: McGraw Hill-Ryerson Ltd., 1985.

Brookfield, Tarah. *Cold War Comforts: Canadian Women, Child Safety, and Global Insecurity, 1945–1975*. Waterloo, ON: Wilfrid Laurier University Press, 2012.

Buckley, Brian. *Gift of Freedom: How Ottawa Welcomed the Vietnamese, Cambodian, and Laotian Refugees*. Renfrew, ON: General Store Publishing House, 2008.

Burns, Jeffrey M. *Disturbing the Peace: A History of the Christian Family Movement, 1949–1974*. Notre Dame, IN: University of Notre Dame Press, 1999.

Casserly, Catherine M. *St. Basil's Parish, 1956–2006: Our Jubilee Journey*. Unpublished manuscript. 2008.

Chesterman, Helen. "The Public Health Nurse and Family Planning," in Dorothy M. Stewart and Pauline A. Vincent, eds. *Public Health Nursing: A Book of Readings*, 165–171. Dubuque, IA: Wm. C. Brown Company Publishers, 1968.

Dalla Costa, Maria, and Selma James. *The Power of Women and the Subversion of the Community*. Bristol, England: Falling Wall Press, 1972.

Daly, Mary. *The Church and the Second Sex*. New York: Harper and Row, 1968.

Davidoff, Leonore *The Best Circles: Society, Etiquette and the Season*. London: Croom Helm, 1973.

Davis, Natalie Zemon. *Society and Culture in Early Modern France: Eight Essays*. Stanford, CA: Stanford University Press, 1975.

Denzin, Norman K. *The Alcoholic Self.* Newbury Park, CA: Sage Publications, 1987.

Deslauriers, Jessie V. *Hotel Dieu Hospital Kingston, 1845–1995.* Kingston, ON: Hotel Dieu Hospital, 1995.

École des Sciences Infirmières de L'université *d'Ottawa 1933-1973 The University of Ottawa School of Nursing.* Ottawa: University of Ottawa Press, 1973.

Elshtain, Jean Bethke, and Sheila Tobias, eds. *Women, Militarism and War.* Savage, MD.: Rowman & Littlefield, 1990.

Freeman, Barbara. "Marion Dewar on Peace, October 30, 1985." Audiotape.

Fullerton Report. *Capital of Canada: How Should It Be Governed? A Special Study on the National Capital.* Ottawa: Information Canada, 1974.

Ganshow, Leonore, Sparks, Richard L. and Javorsky, James (1998) "Foreign Language Learning Difficulties: An Historical Perspective." *Journal of Learning Disabilities*, 31: 248-258.

Gibbon, John Murray. *The Victorian Order of Nurses: 50*th *Anniversary: 1987–1947.* Montreal: The Victorian Order of Nurses for Canada, 1947.

Graham, Katherine A., Susan D. Phillips, with Allan M. Maslove. *Urban Governance in Canada: Representation, Resources, and Restructuring.* Toronto: Harcourt Canada, 1998.

Grant, Bruce. *The Boat People: An 'Age' Investigation.* Harmondsworth, England: Penguin, 1979.

Hamilton, Roberta. *Gendering the Vertical Mosaic: Feminist Perspectives on Canadian Society.* Toronto: Copp Clark, Ltd., 1996.

_____*Setting the Agenda: Jean Royce and the Shaping of Queen's University.* Toronto: University of Toronto Press, 2002.

Heilbrun, Carolyn G. *Writing a Woman's Life*. New York: W. W. Norton & Company, 1988.

Higonnet, Margaret Randolph and Jane Jenson, eds. *Behind the Lines: Gender and the Two World Wars*. New Haven, CT: Yale University Press, 1987.

Kaplan, Harold. *Urban Political Systems: A Functional Analysis of Metro Toronto*. New York: Columbia University Press, 1967.

Kearns, Patricia. "Democracy a la Maude." National Film Board of Canada, 1998.

Kelly, Joan. *Women, History, and Theory: The Essays of Joan Kelly*. Chicago: University of Chicago Press, 1984.

Klein, Bonnie Sher. *Speaking Our Peace*. National Film Board of Canada, 1985.

Kome, Penney. *The Taking of Twenty-Eight: Women Challenge the Constitution*. Toronto: Women's Educational Press, 1983.

Kramarae, Charis and Dale Spender, eds. *Routledge International Encyclopaedia of Women: Global Women's Issues and Knowledge*. London, England: Routledge, 2000.

Kurtz, Ernest. *Not-God: A History of Alcoholics Anonymous*. Center City, MN: Hazelden Educational Services, 1979.

Lam, Lawrence. *From Being Uprooted to Surviving: Resettlement of Vietnamese-Chinese "Boat People" in Montreal, 1980–1990*. Toronto: York Lane Press, 1996.

Lambton, Gunda. *Stealing the Show: Seven Women Artists in Canadian Public Art*. Montreal and Kingston: McGill-Queen's University Press, 1994.

Langrod, George. "Local Government and Democracy" In Lionel D. Feldman and Michael D. Goldrick, eds. *Politics and Government of Urban Canada: Selected Readings*. Second Edition. 4-14. Toronto: Methuen, 1972.

Lapointe, Pierre-Louis. *Buckingham: Au Coeur de la Basse-Lièvre: la ville de Buckingham de ses origines à nos jours, 1824–1990.* Buckingham, QC: Love Printing Services Ltd., 1990.

———. *Buckingham: ville occupée.* Gatineau, QC: Les editions Asticou enrg., 1983.

———. *La vallée assiégee: Buckingam et la Basse Lièvre sous les Maclaren, 1895–1945.* Gatineau, QC: Editions vent de ouest, 2006.

LeSage, E.C. "Policy-Making at City Hall: Ottawa's Office of Equal Opportunity for Women," in Donald G. Rowat, ed. *Urban Politics in Ottawa-Carleton, Research Essays,* Second Edition. 183–207. Ottawa: Department of Political Science, Carleton University, 1983.

Makela, Klaus et al, *Alcoholics Anonymous as a Mutual-Help Movement: A Study in Eight Societies.* Madison: University of Wisconsin Press, 1996.

Mainardi, Pat. "The Politics of Housework," in Robin Morgan, ed. *Sisterhood is Powerful.* New York: Vintage Books, 1970.

Malka, Susan Gelfand. *Daring to Care: American Nursing and Second-Wave Feminism.* Urbana, IL: University of Illinois Press, 2007.

Maron, Edward. *U.S. Catholic,* vol. 34, no. 5, 1968: 21–24.

McKenzie, Judith. *Pauline Jewett: A Passion for Canada.* Montreal & Kingston: McGill-Queen's University Press, 1999.

McLaughlin, Audrey with Rick Archibald. *A Woman's Place: My Life and Politics.* Toronto: Macfarlane Walter & Ross, 1992.

McPherson, Kathryn M. *Bedside Matters: The Transformation of Canadian Nursing, 1900–1990.* Toronto and New York: Oxford University Press, 1996.

Mazigh, Monia. *Hope & Despair: My Struggle to Free My Husband, Maher Arar*. Translated by Patricia Claxton and Fred A. Reed. Toronto: McClelland & Stewart, 2008.

Millett, Kate. *Sexual Politics*. New York: Doubleday & Co., 1970.

Mitchell, Margaret. *No Laughing Matter: Adventure, Activism & Politics*. Vancouver, BC: Granville Island Publishing, 2008.

Munro, Robert C. and Janet M. Medelko, *Electric Reduction Company: Canada's First Chemical Company, 1897–1987*. 2003.

Neuwirth, Gertrud and John Harp. "Civic Sponsorship and Southeast Asian Refugees." Unpublished paper, n.d. 1979.

O'Connell, Dorothy. *Chicklet Gomez*. Ottawa: Deneau & Greenberg, 1978.

Piketty, Thomas. *Capital in the Twenty-First Century*. Translated by Arthur Goldhammer. Cambridge, MA: Harvard University Press, 2014.

Rankin, Joan. *Meet Me at the Chateau: A Legacy of Memory*. Toronto: Heritage Books, 1990.

Ruether, Rosemary Radford, ed. *Religion & Sexism: Images of Women in the Jewish and Christian Traditions*. New York: Simon and Schuster, 1974.

Ruddick, Sara. "Towards a Feminist Peace Politics," in Miriam Cooke and Angela Woollacott, eds. *Gendering War Talk*, 109–127. Princeton, NJ: Princeton University Press, 1993.

Sangster, Joan. "Doing Two Jobs: The Wage-Earning Mother, 1945–1970" in Joy Parr, ed. *A Diversity of Women: Ontario, 1945–1980*, 98–134. Toronto: University of Toronto Press, 1995.

Sewell, John. *Up Against City Hall*. Toronto: James Lewis & Samuel, 1972.

Siegel, David. "Municipal Reform in Ontario: Revolutionary Evolution," in Joseph Garcea and Edward C. LeSage Jr, eds. *Municipal Reform in Canada: Reconfiguration, Re-Empowerment, and Rebalancing*, 127–148. Toronto: Oxford University Press Canada, 2005.

Siegel, Linda S. "Perspectives on Dyslexia." *Journal of Paediatrics and Child Health*. 11(9) (2006): 581–587.

Socnat, Thomas. "Conscientious Objectors in the Context of Canadian Peace Movements." *Journal of Mennonite Studies*, vol 25 (2007): 61–74.

Steinman, Ron. *Inside Television's First War*. Columbia, MO: University of Missouri, 2002.

Stuart, Meryn. "Shifting Professional Boundaries: Gender Conflict in Public Health, 1920–1925," in Dianne Dodd and Deborah Gorham, eds. *Caring and Curing: Historical Perspectives on Women and Healing in Canada*. 49–70. Ottawa: University of Ottawa Press, 1994.

Tallen, Bette S. "Codependency: A Feminist Critique." in Marguerite Babcock and Christine McKay eds. *Challenging Codependency: Feminist Critiques*. 169–176. Toronto: University of Toronto Press, 1995.

Taylor, Eva and James Kennedy. *Ottawa's Britannia*. Ottawa: The Britannia Historical Association, 1983.

Taylor, John H. *Ottawa: An Illustrated History*. Toronto: James Lorimer & Company, 1986.

Tepper, Elliott, ed. *Southeast Asian Exodus: From Tradition to Resettlement*. Ottawa: Canadian Asian Studies Association, 1980.

Threlfall, Richard E. *The Story of 100 Years of Phosphorus Making, 1851–1951*. Oldbury, UK: Albright & Wilson, Ltd, 1951.

Thomas, Owen. "Voter Turnout at the Municipal Level," in Donald G. Rowat, ed. *Urban Politics in Ottawa-Carleton, Research Essays*, Second Edition. 61–82. Ottawa: Department of Political Science, Carleton University, 1983.

Van Esterik, Penny. "Cultural Factors Affecting the Adjustment of Southeast Asian Refugees," in Elliott L. Tepper ed. *Southeast Asian Exodus: From Tradition to Resettlement.* 151–171. Ottawa: Canadian Asian Studies Association 1980.

Vickers, Jill, Pauline Rankin and Christine Appelle. *Politics as if Women Mattered: A Political Analysis of the National Action Committee on the Status of Women.* Toronto: University of Toronto Press, 1993.

Weikart, Lynne A. "Politics and the State: North America." Cheris Kramarae and Dale Spender, eds. *Routledge International Encyclopaedia of Women: Global Women's Issues and Knowledge*, Vol 3: 1599–1603. London: Routledge, 2000.

Whitney, Susan B. *Mobilizing Youth: Communists and Catholics in Interwar France.* Durham, NC: Duke University Press, 2009.

Zajdow, Grazyna. *Al-Anon Narratives, Women, Self-Stories, and Mutual Aid.* Westport, CT: Greenwood Press, 2002.

Controller Dewar square-dancing
at City Hall, c. 1977.

INDEX

2 Driveway, 38, 43

*A Cultural History of the
Nurse's Uniform*, 28–29
*A Woman's Place: My Life and
Politics*, 120, 123
AA. *See* Alcoholics
Anonymous
Abortion Caravan, 5
abortion, 4, 5, 6, 7, 33, 49,
53–54, 72–74, 118, 139
Action Life, 73–74
Ad Hoc Conference, 98–99
Adamson, Nancy, 4
advocacy for women, 97–98
Akeson, Aline, 71
Al-Anon, 39, 41–43
Alcoholics Anonymous (AA),
39, 41–43
Amiel, Barbara, 89
Anderson, Doris, 99
Andrew, Caroline, 74–75,
136–137

Appelle, Christine, 4
Arar, Maher, 128–130
Atkey, Ron, 85
Axworthy, Lloyd, 99

Backhouse, Constance, 101–102
Baglow, John, 73
Bank of Nova Scotia, 26
Barlow, Maude, 98, 100–102,
137
Barrett, Dave, 120
Barry's Bay, 45
Bashevkin, Sylvia, 127–128, 136
Basilian order, 49–50
Baslaw, Morton, 104
Bates, Christina, 28–29
Beaulieu, Aurora, Sister, 29
Belanger, Thomas, 15
Bell family social standing,
16–17, 19, 20, 37–38, 63
Bell, Ada, 12, 17
Bell, Berniad (Bernard), 17
Bell, Hilda, 12, 17

Bell, Marion, pursuit of science, 20, 23, 25, 97. *See also* Dewar, Marion

Bell, Olive, 11, 17, 18, 19, 20, 21, 22–23, 25, 26–27, 37–38, 46, 54

Bell, William, 17

Bell, Wilson Edward, 11–20, 21, 22–23, 25, 42, 44–45, 47, 63

Bell, Wilson (Ted) Edward *III*, 11, 12, 13, 16, 17, 18, 19, 20, 21, 25, 26–27, 37–38, 40

Berndt, Florence Stoodley, 19–20, 26, 32, 33, 37

Bertrand, Giselle, 48

birth control. *See* contraception

Birthright, 72–73

Bisson, Roberta, 27

Black Maria, the, 28

Block system of nursing, 28

Board of Control of Ottawa, 67, 68, 74–75, 103

boat people. *See* refugees

Boston Lying-In Hospital, 32

Breakspear, Alan, 87, 89

Briskin, Linda, 4

Broadbent, Ed, 8, 118, 119, 120, 124

Brodie, Janine, 65–66

Buckingham High School, 23–26

Buckingham Hospital. *See* L'Hôpital St-Michel de Buckingham

Buckingham Post, 37

Buckingham (Quebec), 6, 13–17, 20, 22, 25, 26, 32, 37–38, 45, 47

Byward Market, 107–108

Camp Tekakwitha, 45

Canada Post, 117

Canadian Advisory Council on the Status of Women, 99

Canadian Grill, 32

Carleton University, 128, 130

Carlingwood Ski Hill program, 71

Carter, Rodney, 28

Casserly, Catherine, 55

Cassidy, Michael, 68, 69, 116, 117

Catholic Church, 6–7, 73

Causeway, 97

CFM. *See* Christian Family Movement

Chalice and the Blade: Our History, Our Future, The, 54–55

Chamorro, Pedro Joaquin, 139

Chamorro, Violetta, 139

Charlton, Brian, 117, 119

Charlton, Jean, 117

Charlton, John, 117

Chateau Laurier Hotel, 32

Chesterman, Helen, 57–58

Christian Family Movement (CFM), 51–52, 55

Coatbridge, 12

Cohen, Leah, 102

"Company of Artists and Patrons" portfolio, 103

compassion, 1, 38, 51, 123

contraception (birth control), issue of, 6, 7, 33, 49, 53, 57, 72, 118, 139

"convent, the." *See* École St. Laurent

Copps, Sheila, 124
Cotman, Bernadette, 29–30
Council of the Regional
Municipality of Ottawa-
Carleton, 67
Cunningham (Bell), Agnes,
11–20, 21, 22–23, 25–26, 32, 37,
42–43
Cunningham, Bridget (Cissie),
12, 17, 19
Cunningham, Ellen (Nellie),
12, 17, 19, 25, 44–45

Daly, Mary, 7
Davidoff, Leonore, 16
de Chardin, Pierre Teilhard, 54
Deans, Ian, 117
Dewar cottage, 26–27, 44
Dewar, Catherine (Cathy), 26,
43–49, 53
Dewar, Elizabeth (Liz), 12, 26,
32, 43–46, 53, 115, 130, 135, 137
Dewar, Kenneth (Ken), 6,
31–33, 37–39, 41–49, 49–51, 53,
54, 66, 68, 84–85, 121, 130, 138
Dewar, Kenneth (Ken), as
alcoholic, 39–43, 47
Dewar, Maeghan, 126
Dewar, Marion, as advocate
for peace, 1, 80, 81, 82, 83,
91–97, 108, 123, 127, 135
Dewar, Marion, as alderman,
7–8, 66–68, 70, 74, 103, 108
Dewar, Marion, as controller,
68–72, 74, 75, 106, 108
Dewar, Marion, as deputy
mayor, 68, 72, 73–74, 106

Dewar, Marion, as feminist,
2–3, 6, 39, 55, 58, 82, 95–97, 119,
122, 136
Dewar, Marion, as mayor, 1,
2, 8, 42, 52, 53, 68, 70, 74, 75,
79–108, 115, 116, 121, 135, 136,
137
Dewar, Marion, as member
of Ottawa-Carleton Police
Services Board, 128
Dewar, Marion, as member/
president of New Democratic
Party (NDP), 1–2, 63–66, 70,
79, 89, 100, 115–117, 119, 120,
121, 124, 127
Dewar, Marion, as MP for
Hamilton-Mountain, 2,
117–119, 121, 123, 124
Dewar, Marion, as nurse, 6, 7,
26–33, 39, 42, 50, 55–58, 63, 66,
70, 80, 97, 123, 130
Dewar, Marion, as public
figure, 2, 7, 42, 46, 51, 55,
63–75, 108, 115, 128, 137, 139
Dewar, Marion, as supporter
of the arts, 1, 102–106, 128
Dewar, Marion, Catholic faith,
2, 6–7, 12, 20, 22, 23, 25, 26, 29,
33, 37–38, 41, 44, 45, 49–55, 57,
72, 127, 138–139
Dewar, Marion, growing up in
Buckingham, 13–16
Dewar, Paul, 43–48, 49, 53, 54,
55, 79, 88, 115
Dewar, Robert (Bob), 6, 26,
38–39, 42, 43–48, 51, 53, 54, 62,
68, 79, 126

Dewar's parents' early years, 11–13

disarmament, 1, 80, 82–83, 91–96

discussion and dialogue in Dewar family, 19, 26, 43, 46, 48, 53

Dofasco plant, sexual harassment at, 117–118, 119

Doucet, Clive, 94–95

Downey, Tim, 28

Durr, Pat, 104

dyslexia in Dewar family, 46–47

Echenberg, Havi, 80–81, 85, 139

École St. Laurent ("the convent"), 22–23

Eddy, Corbin, Father, 52, 53, 130–131

Eisler, Riane, 54–55

Electric Reduction Corporation (ERCO), 23, 14–16

Elton, Elizabeth, 90

ERCO. *See* Electric Reduction Corporation

Eugene, Paul, Sister, 33

feminism, 2–4, 5, 7, 57–58, 72, 95–97, 101–102, 124–125, 136–137, 138

feminism, second wave, 3, 5, 138

Feminist Organizing for Change, 4

First Nations people, 1, 82

Florence Nightingale Pledge, 30

Fox, Robert, 48, 53, 54, 80, 91, 104, 128

Frankl, Victor, 54

Franklin, Ursula, 96

Freeman, Barbara, 91, 93, 96–97

French, as language, 12, 17, 22, 33, 47

Frith, Gail, 17, 22–23, 25, 54, 130

Gaffney, Loretta, Sister, 29

Gamble, Barbara, 86

Gamble, Dan, 86, 88

gays and lesbians, rights of, 1, 82

gender roles, 20–25, 41, 46–47, 101, 119, 124

General Electric Company, 11

General Proficiency Medal, 30

Gerber, Don, Rabbi, 87

Gigantes, Evelyn, 66, 69, 84, 97, 100, 116, 135

Gilligan, Carol, 7

Glatt, Harvey, 104

Glatt, Louise, 104

Glebe Collegiate Institute, 6, 25, 26

global vs. local action, 1, 80, 81–82, 91, 94–95, 97, 136

Globe and Mail, The, 120

Goldring, Philip, 44

Gow School, 46

Great Canadian Theatre Company, 104

Greenberg, Lorry, 68, 72, 75, 79

Grey Nuns. *See* Soeurs Grise

Grey, Jerry, 103

Gzowski, Peter, 64

Hamilton-Mountain, 2, 117, 119, 121, 124
Hamilton, Roberta, 3, 4
Harb, Mac, 127
A Love Affair with Politics: A Portrait of Marion Dewar, 127
Harris, Mike, 82, 128
Heilbrun, Carolyn, 124–125
Henighan, Tom, 104–106
Herizons, 99
Holtom, Donna, 85–86, 91, 106
Holy Family Church, 11
Hotel Dieu Hospital in Kingston, 6, 27, 30, 31
Hotel Dieu in Montreal, 27
House of Commons, 118, 120, 121–125
housing, 1, 65, 70–71, 82, 107, 122, 136

Immaculata High School, 73–74
Immigration Act of 1976, 88, 122
In a Different Voice, 7
influence of gender and religion, 20–25
Interval House, 71
invasion of Grenada, denouncing of, 92
Irving, Gordon, Father, 52

Jeanne Mance Pledge, 30
Jewett, Pauline, 63–65, 100, 120, 124

Kehoe, Toddy, 46, 72–73, 80, 100, 115
Kennedy, Trip, 75
Kent, Darrel, 80, 115
Kimmerly, Kenneth, 25
Kingston Whig Standard, 30
Kingston, 6, 27, 30, 31
Klein, Bonnie Sher, 96

L'Hôpital St-Michel de Buckingham (Buckingham Hospital), 32–33
Laforce, Bruce, 23
Lansdowne Park rally, 85–88, 90
Lapointe, Jean Louis, 14–15
le Caine, Trudi, 104
Le, Can, 85, 87, 88, 89
Lewis, Stephen, 70
Liberals, the, 64, 65, 99, 105, 118
Lièvre river and valley, 13, 15
Lowden, Elizabeth, 29
Loyer, Marie, 56–58
Lubbock, Michael, 89

MacDonald, Flora, 88, 118, 127
MacKenzie, David, 119
MacLaren family and enterprise, 13–16
Macphail, Agnes, 125
MacSween, Donald, 105
MAG. *See* Mayor's Advisory Group on Arts and Culture
Mainardi, Pat, 138
Malka, Susan Gelfand, 7, 58
Man's Search for Meaning, 54

Mance, Jeanne, 27
Mao, Chairman, 96
marriage to Kenneth Dewar,
38–39, 41–43, 48
Marshall, Kay, 62
Marshall, Peter, 62
Masson (Quebec), 13, 15, 16, 17
Mayor's Advisory Group on
Arts and Culture (MAG),
104–105
Mazigh, Monia, 128–130
McDougall, Barbara, 118
McGill University, 26
McGonnigal, Mary Jane, 31,
32, 37–38, 40
McLaughlin, Audrey, 2, 114,
117, 120–121, 123–124, 127
McPhail, Margaret, 4
McPherson, Kathryn, 27
Millett, Kate, 3, 137–138
Mills, Russell, 86, 90
Milner, Arthur, 102, 104
Mitchell, Margaret, 100, 125
Montreal, 11, 12, 13, 17
Morris, Elaine, 48–49

NAC. *See* National Action
Committee on the Status of
Women
National Action Committee
on the Status of Women
(NAC), 4
National Arts Centre, 103, 105
National Capital Commission,
66–67
National Research Council
(NRC), 93

NDP. *See* New Democratic
Party
Nemiroff, Greta Hofmann, 2,
16, 19, 39, 55, 121, 124
Nepean High School, 25
nepotism, 82, 101, 135
Neve, Alex, 128–130
New Democratic Party (NDP),
65, 66, 70, 79, 116–117, 120–121,
123–124, 127, 128
Newspaper Guild, 71–72
Nichol, Pat, 75, 79, 80
NRC. *See* National Research
Council
nursing, 7, 26–30, 55–58, 70

O'Connell, Dorothy, 70–71
Office of Equal Opportunity
for the City of Ottawa, 100, 137
Ontario Medical Association,
58
Order of Canada, 8, 130
ordination of women, 7, 49, 53,
54, 139
Ottawa Citizen, 66, 68, 79, 86
Ottawa Civic Hospital, 6, 31,
32, 42
Ottawa General Hospital's
School of Nursing, 26
Ottawa Journal, 71–72, 74, 86
Ottawa police station, 103–104
Ottawa River, 13, 26–27
Ottawa Tenants Council for
Public Housing, 70–71
Ottawa Women's Bookstore,
97
Ottawa Women's Centre, 72–73

Ottawa Women's Credit
Union, 98
Ottawa, 1, 5, 6, 8, 13, 19, 22, 25,
26, 31, 32, 38–49, 51, 52, 62–63,
66–68, 71–73, 74–75, 79, 82–84,
90–91, 93, 97, 98–99, 100,
102–103, 104–108
Our Lady of Victory Church,
25, 37–38
Oxfam Canada, 128

Padolsky, Barry, 106–108
Phinny, Beth, 118
Pilon, Debra, 99
Planned Parenthood
Federation, 118
Plourde (Ottawa), Archbishop,
54, 87
"Politics of Housework, The,"
138
poor, the, 1, 27, 71, 79
Pope John Paul II, 50
Pope John XXIII, 6
pornography, dangers of, 122
Project 4000, 1, 83–91
public health, 55–57, 67
"Public Health Nurse and
Family Planning, The," 57–58
public transportation, 1, 65,
68, 136

Queen's University, 20, 25, 27,
30, 63–64, 97
question period at House of
Commons, 121–124, 128

Rae, Bob, 117, 120, 128

Rankin, Pauline, 4
Red Cross, 16, 17
refugees (including the "boat
people"), 1, 83–91, 122, 135
"Refuse the Cruise"
demonstration, 93–94
Registered Nurses Association
of Ontario qualifying
examination, 31
Reid, Don, 75
Religious Hospitallers Award,
30
Religious Hospitallers of St.
Joseph, 27
Renwick, Norah Cassidy, 22
"Respect for Life" Day, 73–74
Rex Avenue, 43, 46, 48, 50–51
Rideau Centre, the, 83,
106–108
Rideau Street Convent, 22
Rideau Street Public Advisory
Committee, 107
Rideau Street, 107–108
Roberts, Wayne Wendell, 23
Robinson, William, Anglican
Bishop, 87
Rockliffe Park, 19
Royal Commission on the
Status of Women, 3–4, 5
Royce, Jean, 64
Ruddick, Sarah, 95–96
Ruth, Anthony John, Father,
49–51, 54
Ryan, Eleanor, 89

Sand Point, 26–27, 44
Scott, F.R., 66

Second Vatican Council, 6, 49,
51, 54
Section 252 of the Criminal
Code, 118
Section 28 of the Canadian
Charter of Rights and
Freedoms; Twenty-Eight,
98–100
setting out of her vocation,
30–33
Seven Sisters Hydro-Electric
Dam, 11, 13
Sewell, John, 82
sexual harassment, 101–102, 119
Sexual Politics, 3, 137–138
Shock Doctrine, 129
Socknat, Thomas, 93
Soeurs Grise (Grey Nuns),
22, 32
Speaking Our Peace, 96
St. Basil's Church, 7, 49–51, 53,
56, 121, 130
St. Basil's Social Action
Committee, 51, 55
St. Dominic's Parish, 13
St. Gregory's. *See* St.-Grégoire
de Naziance
St. James's Club, 19
St. Joseph's School of Nursing,
6, 27–30, 31
St. Mary's of the Lake
Hospital, 28
St. Patrick's High School, 31
St.-Grégoire de Naziance (St.
Gregory's), 22, 49
steelworkers of Hamilton-
Mountain, 119

Sullivan, Father, 28, 30
Sutherland, Ralph, 66

Tallen, Bette, 39
Taylor, Susan Geraldine, 103
Temple, Israel, 87
Theatre Ballet of Canada, 104
Todd, Allan, 15–16
Toeing the Lines, 127–128
Trudeau, Pierre, 64, 99, 103

University of Ottawa, 6, 57,
62, 63
Up Against City Hall, 82
upward mobility: becoming
pillars of the community,
16–20

Vancouver Women's Caucus, 5
Vancouver, 5
Vickers, Jill, 4, 65, 121, 127
Victorian Order of Nurses
(VON), 6, 57, 58
visible minorities, 1, 117
VON. *See* Victorian Order of
Nurses

"Wages for Housework"
movement, 138
Walker, R.B., 23
wedding of Marion Bell and
Kenneth Dewar, 37–38, 40
White, Joan, 51
Whitton, Charlotte, 8
Winnipeg River, 13
Winnipeg, 11–13
Winsor, Hugh, 120

women and the church, 7, 46,
49, 52, 53, 54, 55, 57, 139
women in politics, 2, 66, 68,
97, 100–102, 116, 118, 120–121,
124–125, 127–128, 136
Women's Career Counselling
Centre, 97
women's rights, 1, 3, 5, 6, 7, 46,
54, 72–74, 79, 81, 82, 83, 97–99,
100, 108, 117, 118, 119, 122, 127,
135, 138–139

Young, Lynne, 90

Zajdow, Grazyna, 41

ACKNOWLEDGEMENTS

It was a privilege to work on this biography of Marion Dewar.

I could not have written this book without support and encouragement from Bob, Liz, Cathy, and Paul Dewar, Marion and Ken Dewar's four children. Other extended family members – Ted Bell, Heather Bell, Gail Frith, and Elaine Morris – all kindly agreed to talk to me as well. I knew Paul Dewar first, and I am so grateful for his support and encouragement, but it was Bob Dewar who was my main contact for this project. I thank him for his invaluable and unstinting help.

I am indebted to the expert and generous assistance I received from archivist Signe Jeppesen, Theresa Sorel and other staff members and volunteers at the City of Ottawa Archives.

Many thanks to Rodney Carter, archivist for the Religious Hospitallers of Saint Joseph. The R HSJ were the Sisters responsible for the St. Joseph's School of Nursing at the Hotel Dieu Hospital in Kingston, Ontario.

This book is the result of a collaboration between the Feminist History Society (FHS) and the publisher, Second Story Press. The Feminist History Society's admirable purpose is to encourage the writing of the history of feminism in Canada. I thank Constance Backhouse of the FHS. All the FHS readers were helpful, but most especially Beth Atcheson. I thank Kathryn White, my editor, for her careful and astute reading, her excellent judgement, and her friendship. I could not, however, have dealt with the computer program now used for editing without the help of Beth Robertson, a recent Ph.D. graduate from the Department of History at Carleton University. I am very grateful to her. I also thank Kelly Jones who carefully prepared the Index.

I visited Second Story Press in August 2015. What a great place! It hums with energy. Everyone was warm and welcoming. It is a feminist workplace to celebrate. I thank publisher Margie Wolfe, whose skill and passion have kept the press alive and well for twenty-five years. I thank Kathryn Cole, managing editor, for all her help, Melissa Kaita, production manager and photograph scanning expert, and copy editor Marg Anne Morrison.

I thank Caroline Andrew, John Smart, John Taylor, Brian Buckley, Father Bosco Wong, Mort and the late Nancy Berkovitz, Bob and Linda Cameron, and Valerie Knowles. They all generously talked to me at length, even though I did not conduct formal interviews with them.

I also thank Mark Abley, Denyse Baillargeon, Marilyn Barber, John Brule, Catherine Casserly, Claire Devlin, Dianne Dodd, Jayne Elliot, Barbara Freeman, Aviva Freedman, Mary Garrett, Norman Hillmer, Anthony Keith, Joan Jonkel, Cindy Laverne, Sebastian Levenson, Susan Gelfand Malka (fellow historian and dear sister-in-law), David Mackenzie, Karen March, Bruce Murduck, James Opp, Ellen Herwitz Pollack, Susan Poole, Nancy Renaud, Mel Segal, John Smart, Sako Torrossian and others at Laurier Office Mart, Adnan Turg, Susan Whitney, and Janice Williamson.

In the summer of 2012 when I interviewed Cathy Dewar, her seven-year-old grandson (Treyson Kenneth Dewar) came home from day camp. When his grandmother was out of the room, Treyson sat down across the table from me, looked at me solemnly, and asked, "Why are you talking to my grandmother?"

"Well, I was talking to her about your great-grandmother, who was mayor of Ottawa," I replied.

"I know that," said Treyson. There was a pause and then he said: "Are you going to talk to *everybody* in Ottawa?"

"That might be a good idea, Treyson," I said. "But if I tried to do that, I'd never get finished."

"I understand," he said.

I didn't interview "everybody in Ottawa," but the many oral

interviews I did conduct have added immensely to this book. It was a pleasure and an honour to talk to all of these people, and I thank each of them. Their names and the dates of the interviews are listed in the Appendix.

I thank my son, David Keith, and his family, including his wife Kirsten Anderson Keith, and my grandchildren, Alex and Sarah Keith.

And last but not least, I thank Toby Gelfand, my husband, friend, and fellow historian. He is my most helpful, willing, forthcoming, and supportive critic.

For any remaining errors or omissions, I am, of course, responsible.

PHOTO CREDITS

Cover: Courtesy of the City of Ottawa Archives/MG448-07-018/CA024926/Michael Basham

Page x: Courtesy of the City of Ottawa Archives/RG027/CA991947b

Page 4: Courtesy of the City of Ottawa Archives/MG448-02-22/CA024925

Page 5: Courtesy of the City of Ottawa Archives/MG448-06-010/CA024927

Page 14: Courtesy of Paul Dewar

Page 18: Courtesy of Bob Dewar

Page 21: Courtesy of Bob Dewar

Page 24: Courtesy of Florence Berndt

Page 29: Courtesy of Rodney Carter, Archivist, Hotel Dieu Hospital, Kingston, Ontario.

Page 31: Courtesy of Elizabeth Lowden

Page 38: Courtesy of Bob Dewar

Page 40: Courtesy of Bob Dewar

Page 43: Courtesy of Bob Dewar

Page 44: Courtesy of Bob Dewar

Page 45: Courtesy of Bob Dewar

Page 50: Courtesy of the City of Ottawa Archives/MG448-07-010/C024929

Page 52: Courtesy of Bob Dewar

Page 62: Courtesy of Bob Dewar

Page 69: Courtesy of Bob Dewar

Page 81: Courtesy of the City of Ottawa Archives/MG488-07-012/CA024928

Page 86: Courtesy of Eleanor Ryan

Page 87: Courtesy of Eleanor Ryan

Page 92: Courtesy of the City of Ottawa Archives/ MG448-07-019/CA024924

Page 94: Courtesy of Deborah Gorham

Page 96: Courtesy of the City of Ottawa Archives/ MG448-07-009/CA024930

Page 98: Courtesy of the City of Ottawa Archives/ MG448-07-006/CA024931

Page 114: Courtesy of Bob Dewar

Page 126: Courtesy of Bob Dewar

Page 129: Courtesy of Bob Dewar

Page 152: Courtesy of the City of Ottawa Archives/ MG448-07-006/CA024932/Peter J. Graham

ABOUT THE AUTHOR

DEBORAH GORHAM taught History and Women's Studies at Carleton University for forty years. She set up, planned and taught the first women's history course at the university – one of the first such courses in North America. She retains her connection to Carleton as a Distinguished Research Professor. She is the author of *The Victorian Girl and the Feminine Ideal* (1982, 2013), *Vera Brittain: A Feminist Life* (1996, 2000) and co-editor of *Up and Doing: Canadian Women and Peace* (1989) and *Caring and Curing: Historical Perspectives on Women and Healing in Canada* (1994). Deborah lives in Ottawa.